All-C

Object Lessons Series

Bess, C. W., *Children's Object Sermons for the Seasons,* 1026-8

Bess, C. W., *Object-Centered Children's Sermons,* 0734-8

Bess, C. W., *Sparkling Object Sermons for Children,* 0824-7

Bess, C. W., & Roy DeBrand, *Bible-Centered Object Sermons for Children,* 0886-7

Biller, Tom & Martie, *Simple Object Lessons for Children,* 0793-3

Bruinsma, Sheryl, *Easy-to-Use Object Lessons,* 0832-8

Bruinsma, Sheryl, *More Object Lessons for Very Young Children,* 1075-6

Bruinsma, Sheryl, *New Object Lessons,* 0775-5

Bruinsma, Sheryl, *Object Lessons for Every Occasion,* 0994-4

Bruinsma, Sheryl, *Object Lessons for Special Days,* 0920-0

Bruinsma, Sheryl, *Object Lessons for Very Young Children,* 0956-1

Bruinsma, Sheryl, *Object Lessons Using Children's Toys,* 5695-0

Claassen, David, *Object Lessons for a Year,* 2514-1

Connelly, H. W., *47 Object Lessons for Youth Programs,* 2314-9

Coombs, Robert, *Concise Object Sermons for Children,* 2541-9

Coombs, Robert, *Enlightening Object Lessons for Children,* 2567-2

Cooper, Charlotte, *50 Object Stories for Children,* 2523-0

Cross, Luther, *Easy Object Stories,* 2502-8

Cross, Luther, *Object Lessons for Children,* 2315-7

Cross, Luther, *Story Sermons for Children,* 2328-9

De Jonge, Joanne, *More Object Lessons from Nature,* 3004-8

De Jonge, Joanne, *Object Lessons from Nature,* 2989-9

De Jonge, Joanne, *Object Lessons from Pebbles and Paper Clips,* 5041-3

De Jonge, Joanne, *Object Lessons from Your Home and Yard,* 3026-9

Edstrom, Lois, *Contemporary Object Lessons for Children's Church,* 3432-9

Gebhardt, Richard, & Mark Armstrong, *Object Lessons from Science Experiments,* 3811-1

Godsey, Kyle, *Object Lessons About God,* 3841-3

Hendricks, William, *Object Lessons Based on Bible Characters,* 4373-5

Hendricks, William, & Merle Den Bleyker, *Object Lessons from Sports and Games,* 4134-1

Hendricks, William, & Merle Den Bleyker, *Object Lessons That Teach Bible Truths,* 4172-4

Loeks, Mary, *Object Lessons for Children's Worship,* 5584-9

McDonald, Roderick, *Successful Object Sermons,* 6270-5

Runk, Wesley, *Object Lessons from the Bible,* 7698-6

Squyres, Greg, *Simple Object Lessons for Young Children,* 8330-3

Sullivan, Jessie, *Object Lessons and Stories for Children's Church,* 8037-1

Sullivan, Jessie, *Object Lessons with Easy-to-Find Objects,* 8190-4

Trull, Joe, *40 Object Sermons for Children,* 8831-3

All-Occasion Object Lessons

Joanne E. De Jonge

BakerBooks
A Division of Baker Book House Co
Grand Rapids, Michigan 49516

ISBN 0-8010-5690-X

This book is dedicated to
the Lord of all occasions.

Contents

Introduction

You can use this versatile book on special occasions and on any occasion. For *special* occasions, check the table of contents. All special occasions are listed in parentheses behind the lesson titles.

Special-occasion lessons do not teach about special days; they use the occasion to teach biblical truths. Society bombards our children with symbols of special (often contrived) days. These lessons link those symbols to a truth so that our children will be bombarded with truths.

For *any* occasion, use almost any lesson. Most special-occasion lessons contain options; you can use them for general occasions or for the special occasion listed.

Would you like a seasonal lesson? Lessons have been arranged to correspond roughly to the calendar year.

Do you wish to highlight a particular passage of Scripture? Verses used are listed directly below each lesson title at the beginning of the chapter.

Do you wish to teach a certain concept? The concept of each lesson is stated directly below the Scripture citation at the beginning of the chapter.

Are you unable to think of an object and are short of time? Some of these lessons use no objects other than the children or the congregation. Most of the lessons use objects that you'll find nearby. Even special-occasion lessons use objects that you can hardly avoid at certain seasons.

Do you want to reach a child who responds to extraordinary stimuli? Some lessons use shapes, colors, sounds, or actions to make a point.

Do you lack self-confidence? These lessons are complete as written. You can give them word for word and follow the "stage directions" printed in parentheses.

Are you a seasoned presenter looking for a few new ideas? These lessons are adaptable. Peruse them for ideas; you'll find some unique pairings of common objects and biblical truths.

Take some time to page through this book. You'll find it a versatile, useful set of object lessons for all occasions.

1

Peanut-Butter-and-Jelly Kids

Scripture: Man looks at the outward appearance, but the LORD looks at the heart (1 Sam. 16:7).

Concept: God cares about what's in our hearts.

Objects: A peanut-butter-and-jelly sandwich and a sardine sandwich. (You can use any two sandwiches, one that most children like and one that they dislike. Simply change the names of the sandwiches in the text.)

I brought two sandwiches with me today. *(Hold up the sandwiches.)* I'd like to know which sandwich you would like best.

(Hold up the peanut-butter-and-jelly sandwich. Open it so the children can see the contents.) This is a peanut-butter-and-jelly sandwich. How many of you like peanut-butter-and-jelly sandwiches? *(Pause for response.)* I think almost everyone does. Peanut-butter-and-jelly is a real favorite. *(Hold up the sandwich.)* So, most of you would like this sandwich, right? *(Nod and pause for response.)*

Here's another sandwich. *(Hold up the sardine sandwich. Open it so the children can see the contents.)* This is a sardine sandwich. There are stinky little fish *(or*

11

whatever you use) in this sandwich. How many would like this sandwich? *(Pause for response.)* No one wants a sardine sandwich?

I offered you two different kinds of sandwiches. Lots of people like peanut-butter-and-jelly, but not many wanted the sardine sandwich.

Yet they're both sandwiches. They look alike—two slices of bread with something between. What's the difference? Why do you like peanut-butter-and-jelly sandwiches and not sardine sandwiches? *(Pause for response.)* Of course! What we put inside the sandwich makes all the difference in the world. The bread holds the sandwich together, but it's what's inside that counts.

That's just like people. Or maybe we could say that people are just like sandwiches; it's what's inside that counts.

God says that your appearance doesn't matter at all to him. You can be fat or skinny, short or tall, good-looking or not; that makes no difference to God. That's only your outside. *(Hold up the sandwich.)* Your appearance is like the bread that holds a sandwich together.

The good stuff's inside. *(Open a sandwich.)* Here's what counts. And here *(point to your heart)* is what counts to God. This *(point to your heart)* is where there is love, and kindness, and goodness. This *(point to your heart)* is what matters to God.

The Bible tells us that, while people may look at our appearance, God looks at our hearts. It's what's inside of us that matters to God.

12

Do you love Jesus? Do you want to be a kind, loving person? *(Hold up the peanut-butter-and-jelly sandwich.)* Then you're like a good sandwich. You've got good stuff inside, and that's what counts.

The next time someone makes a sandwich for you, maybe you'll ask for peanut butter and jelly, or something else good. *(Hold up a sandwich and point to your heart.)* And that good sandwich can remind you that it's what's inside that counts. God cares about what's in your heart.

Put On a Little Gentleness

Scripture: Be completely humble and gentle; be patient, bearing with one another in love (Eph. 4:2).

Concept: We should consciously try to be humble and gentle.

Object: A container of hand lotion.

Can anyone tell me what this is? *(Show the children the hand lotion and pause for response.)* That's right, it's hand lotion. I use a lot of lotion during the winter; I think many people do. Our skin becomes really dry, so we put on hand lotion to make it nice and smooth again.

Sometimes, when you play outside in the cold weather, your hands or your cheeks become dry, chapped, and rough. *(Show the children the lotion.)* Then you must put some lotion on your hands or cheeks to make them nice and smooth again.

How many of you have had dry or chapped hands or cheeks? *(Pause for response.)* Chapped cheeks and hands can really hurt, can't they? *(Nod your head and pause for response.)*

Nobody likes his or her cheeks and hands to feel dry and rough. So we put on a little lotion *(put a lit-*

tle lotion on your hands and rub it in; continue to speak as you do so) to make them nice and smooth again.

There's another part of us that should be smooth and kind and gentle instead of rough and harsh. Our personality—the way we act and what we say—should be smooth, gentle, and kind. In the Bible, God tells us to be gentle.

How can you be gentle with people? *(Pause for response. Repeat the children's responses. You may have to prompt them with questions.)* When you play with someone, do you boss them around, or do you play nicely together? Do you grab the toys you want, or do you share? Do you push your way to the front of a line, or do you wait your turn? Do you yell at people, or do you talk softly? Do you say mean things to people, or do you find nice things to say? Do you tease kids younger than you, or do you help them?

You get the idea; there are all sorts of ways to be gentle. But it isn't always easy, is it? *(Shake your head and pause for response.)* No! Sometimes we'd rather not share, or we'd like to boss someone; sometimes it's hard to be gentle.

But God tells us to be gentle, so we should try really hard to speak gently and act gently. We should try to keep those harsh, rough words or actions under control.

(Show the children the lotion again.) Trying to be gentle is just like trying to keep our chapped, rough cheeks and hands nice and smooth. It takes a little work. *(Put a little lotion on your hands again and rub it in. Continue to speak as you do so.)* You must remem-

ber to put the lotion on and rub it in. I do this almost every day in the winter.

Also, almost every day, I try to remember to be gentle. Just as I keep my hands smooth, I try to keep myself gentle. So, I'll rub in the lotion and remind myself to be gentle today.

Option

(If not too many children are in front, you may want to include this paragraph.)

Would you like a little bit of lotion? *(Hold up the bottle and pause for response.)* I'll give each of you just a little bit if you hold out your hands. You can rub it in on your way back to your seats. *(Put a little lotion into each child's cupped hands. Continue to speak as you do so.)*

Continue Lesson

You can try to do the same thing this week. Rub a little lotion—just a little bit—onto your hands or cheeks every day to keep them soft and smooth. And, as you do, remind yourself always to keep your actions and your words gentle. God wants us to be gentle people.

3

Your Very Best Valentine

(Valentine's Day)

Scripture: For God so loved the world that he gave his one and only Son, that whoever believes in him shall not perish but have eternal life (John 3:16).

Concept: God loves you.

Objects: A red paper heart for each child. (*Note:* This lesson can be used anytime as written. For Valentine's Day, use option 1.)

Option 1

(Use these paragraphs before Valentine's Day.)

Who can tell me what this is? *(Hold up one of the hearts and pause for response.)* Yes, it's a heart. It's a valentine.

How many of you have seen valentines lately? *(Pause for response.)* Yes, I think we all have. Next (the day) will be Valentine's Day, so stores are selling lots of valentines. Most valentines are shaped like a heart or have a heart on them. *(Hold up the heart again.)*

Valentine's Day is all about love. That's the day people say "I love you" to other people. Of course, we love people all year; but some people like to use a special day to talk about love in a special way.

That's why people like valentines. *(Hold up a few hearts.)* A valentine *reminds* the person who gets it that somebody loves him or her.

How many of you are going to give away a valentine or two? *(Pause for response.)* It's fun to give valentines, isn't it? We should show people we love them throughout the year; but it's also nice to give a valentine *reminder* that we love them.

How many of you think that you're going to *get* a valentine? *(Pause for response. How you respond will depend on the response. If all the children indicate they will receive a valentine, say,)* You are all right! I'm sure you all will receive valentines, because I have one for each of you. *(If some children think they will not receive a valentine, say,)* Some people think that they won't receive any valentines, but they're wrong. I have a valentine for each of you.

(Pass out one heart to each child, personally. Continue to speak as you do so.) This valentine is the very best valentine that you'll receive this year or any year. It's not very fancy. Look at it closely. It's only a red paper heart; that's it. It's not very big, and there's no decoration on it. It doesn't look much like the valentines you see in stores. Are there any words on it? *(Pause for response.)* No! There's nothing written on it. It's only a small paper heart. *(Continue to comment on the hearts until every child has one.)*

Option 2

(Use these paragraphs anytime.)

Who can tell me what this is? *(Hold up one of the hearts and pause for response.)* Yes, it's a heart. What does a heart stand for? *(Pause for response.)* Of course, a heart stands for love. A heart is a *reminder* of love.

People often use hearts to stand for love. Sometimes you can find hearts in birthday cards or other cards. They mean, "I love you." Sometimes you may see a heart with letters written inside of it. That usually means "So-and-so loves so-and-so." Sometimes adults send cards with hearts to other adults just to say "I love you." They just want to *remind* each other that they love each other.

Has anyone here ever received a birthday card with hearts on it? *(Pause very slightly.)* You probably don't remember, do you? Has anyone here ever received a heart-shaped card that said "I love you"? *(Pause for response.)* Maybe someday you'll receive a card like that. How many of you think that you will receive a heart card someday? *(Pause for response.)* You probably haven't thought about that much yet.

I know that each of you will receive an "I love you" heart. In fact, you will get one today, because I have one for each of you.

(Give one heart to each child. Continue to speak as you do so.) This is the very best heart card that you'll ever receive. It's not very fancy. Look at it closely. It's only a red paper heart. There's nothing written on it. But it's still the best heart that you'll ever get.

Continue Lesson

Remember that I said a heart is a *reminder* of someone's love? It doesn't have to be fancy to tell you someone loves you. Just look at the heart and it reminds you of love.

This valentine is the best one you'll ever get because it's a reminder that God loves you. Before you were ever born, God loved you. He has promised to love you forever. God will never, ever change his love for you. Nothing can ever separate you from God's love. You are his child and he loves you.

That's wonderful, isn't it? *(Nod your head and pause for response.)* Our great God loves us! He tells us that again and again in the Bible.

(Hold up a heart.) We really don't need reminders like this, do we? All we have to do is look around at everything that God gives us. All we have to do is read our Bibles. All we have to do is think about Jesus to know that God loves us.

Yet, a little paper heart is nice once in a while, isn't it? That's why I gave you one today. Some of you may get many (valentines this week *or* hearts when you grow up) and some of you will receive fewer. But that doesn't matter. *(Hold up a heart.)* You each have the very best heart of all, this reminder that God loves you.

Take this home and put it where you can see it this week. It's your special reminder that God loves you.

4

The Wonder of Life

(Right to Life)

Scripture: For you created my inmost being; you knit me together in my mother's womb (Ps. 139:13).

Concept: Only God can make precious human life; we should respect it.

Object: A baby doll. Try to get as lifelike a doll as possible. (*Note:* This lesson can be used anytime as written. The option for specific right-to-life use is included near the end of the lesson.)

I brought a plaything with me today. I suspect many of you have one of these toys. (*Hold up the doll.*) How many of you have a doll? (*Pause for response.*) How many of you like to play with your doll? (*Pause for response.*)

This doll belongs to (name the doll's owner). I think it's especially nice because it's so lifelike. It's probably fun to play with because it looks so much like a real baby.

(*Point out the lifelike features of the doll. Hold up the doll so that the children can see the feature you mention.*

Make at least one comment about that feature. Finish each comment with, ". . . just like a real baby's _____." *For example, say,)* Look at its eyes! *(Hold the doll so that the children can see its eyes.)* They're brown and they open and close, just like a real baby's eyes.

I like this doll because it looks so much like a real baby. But it isn't real, is it? *(Shake your head and pause briefly.)* What's the difference between this doll and a real baby? *(Pause for response. Repeat responses.)* Of course, this is only a doll; a real baby is alive!

This doll isn't a real person; it doesn't have life. *(Hold the doll in a position you would not hold a baby in, to make its lifelessness obvious.)* This doll won't ever say a single word. It will never *think* a single word. It will never feel sad or happy or scared or safe. It will never feel love. It won't feel or think a thing, because it's only a doll; it isn't alive.

Can we give this doll life? Can we turn it into a real person? *(Pause for response.)* No! It's silly to even think that, isn't it? We can't give life. We can make a doll look like a baby, but we can't give it life and make it into a real baby.

Who's the only person who can give human life? *(Pause for response.)* That's right; only God can give life. The Bible says that God creates our innermost beings— our thoughts, our feelings, our love. God gives us life.

The Bible says that when God knits us together he gives us our innermost being, our life. Before we're born, when we're tiny babies waiting to be born, God has given us life. *How* he gives life is a mystery; only God knows.

For just a minute, look at all the children sitting near you. *(Pause slightly.)* Each one of you is alive. Each one of you thinks and feels and loves. God gave each of you that precious life.

Now take a minute to look at everybody sitting out there. *(Indicate the congregation and pause slightly.)* God gave each person out there that precious life, too. Each person you see thinks and feels and loves and has God-given inner life. (*For option, say,* even some people you can't see yet—tiny babies waiting to be born— have that precious life.) That life is wonderful.

This doll *(hold up the doll)* may look like a real baby. But it's only a doll. You can play with it and pretend it's a baby. You can do whatever you want with your own doll, because it's only a doll.

But a real person is different. We should respect and feel wonder at the life God gives to a real person—old, young, a baby, (*with option say,* even a baby waiting to be born). A person's life is very important.

Option

(Include the following paragraphs if you would like to mention the right to life.)

We all know that life is special and that only God can give life. But sometimes we need reminders about how special life is; adults especially need reminders.

Some adults forget, or don't know, that God made us and gave us life. They don't know that God gave everyone life, even little babies and babies waiting to be born. Sometimes they forget the difference between *(hold up the doll)* dolls and people. Some people don't honor life.

That's why we're talking about life today. You may hear people talk about the right to life. Right-to-Life Day is a reminder that God gives everyone, even babies waiting to be born, life, and we should respect it.

Continue Lesson

Dolls are lots of fun, aren't they? *(Hold up the doll and pause for response.)* Of course, they're fun to play with usually because they're your dolls and you can do almost whatever you want with them.

But all people are different from dolls. People have life that only God can give. That's something very special.

Have fun playing with your dolls. But remember: Always treat real life with respect and wonder. It comes from God.

5

The Color of Life

(St. Patrick's Day)

Scripture: I have come that they may have life, and have it to the full (John 10:10).

Concept: God gives us life.

Objects: A sheet of red paper, a sheet of black paper, a sheet of green paper. Optional: a green plant, a green St. Patrick's Day decoration. (*Note:* This lesson can be used anytime as written. The option for specific St. Patrick's Day use is included near the end of the lesson.)

Today we're going to talk about some different colors. *(Display the red paper.)* What color is this? *(Pause for response.)* Red! How many of you like the color red? *(Pause for response.)* I think red is a happy color. How many of you think red is a happy color? *(Pause for response.)*

Some people don't like red. They think that red is an angry color. Is there anyone here who doesn't like red? *(Pause for response.)* OK. Different people like different colors.

Here's a color that I think is not very happy. Other people may like it. *(Display the black paper.)* Black, for me, is a sad color. How many of you think black is a sad color? *(Pause for response.)*

Of course, some people really like black. They think it matches lots of colors so it's a useful color. How many of you like black? *(Pause for response.)* OK. Different people think different things when they see different colors.

Here's a color that not many people think about, yet we see lots of it. *(Display the green paper.)* How many of you like green? *(Pause for response.)* How many of you don't like green? *(Pause for response.)* How many of you don't care; green's OK but not your favorite color? *(Pause for response.)*

Green is a very special color for me. Shall I tell you why? *(Pause briefly.)* Green makes me happy to be alive.

Let me explain. Grass is green. Trees are green. Bushes are green. *(Hold up the plant, then put it in front of you as you speak.)* All living plants are green. That's the way God made them.

We need green things to stay alive. Green, living plants give us food and healthy air. If we didn't have green plants we wouldn't be alive. That's the way God made us.

So, I'm glad that there's a lot of green in the world. I'm glad that God gave us lots of green plants, because they help keep me alive.

Of course, green plants don't give us life. They *help* us stay alive, but they don't *make* us alive. Who gives us life? *(Pause for response.)* Yes, God does. Only God can give us life. Only God can give anything life. God gives us life, and then God gives us green, living plants.

When I see green *(hold up the green paper),* I think of life, and then I think of God, who gave me life. And I'm happy that God gave me life, so green makes me happy.

Option

(Include the following paragraphs if you would like to mention St. Patrick's Day.)

You'll probably see a lot of green this week. Some people will celebrate St. Patrick's Day. People usually decorate with green for St. Patrick's Day. *(Hold up the decoration.)* You'll probably see things like this in windows and in stores.

This week, when people see green, many will probably think only of one day, St. Patrick's Day. But when you see green, you can think of something much better. You can think of life!

Continue Lesson

This week, I'd like you to look especially for the color green. How many green plants and trees can you find? Is some grass greener than other grass? Are bushes green yet? *(Option:* See how many decorations like this you can find.) And, whenever you see green, think of life. Then think of God, who gives us all life. And thank God for giving you life.

This week, remember that green means life. Thank God for life.

6

Remember Our Sins . . .

(Lent)

Scripture: If we confess our sins, he is faithful and just and will forgive us our sins and purify us from all unrighteousness (1 John 1:9).

Concept: We should confess our sins.

Objects: A small bag of dirt for each child. (*Note:* This lesson should be done in conjunction with ". . . No More!" These lessons can be used anytime as written. The option for specific Lenten use is included near the end of the lesson.)

I brought some dirt with me today—just plain old dirt. (*Open a bag and show the children some of the dirt. Put your hands into it when you show them.*) Dirt is so common, we see it all over the place. In fact, we see dirt so much that we don't really take time to think about it, do we? (*Shake your head and pause for response.*)

That's why I want to talk about it today. Dirt is so common that we forget about it. Sometimes we have to remind ourselves about dirt.

What about dirt? Well, it's dirty, isn't it? (*Hold up the hand that you've had in the dirt.*) Handle dirt and you become dirty.

How many of you have played in dirt and gotten yourselves dirty? *(Pause for response.)* I think that everybody has. Dirt's all over the place; everybody becomes dirty sometimes.

Sometimes, before you go out to play, does an adult say to you, "Don't get too dirty"? Have you ever heard someone say that? *(Pause for response.)* Of course, once in a while we have to remind ourselves to try to stay clean.

That's why I've got a bag of dirt for each of you today. *(Indicate the bags of dirt.)* Your bag of dirt is going to be a special reminder to you this week. Every time you see your bag of dirt, say to yourself, "There's dirt all over the place. I'll try to stay clean. If I don't, I'll wash myself well." Can you remember to say that this week? *(Nod and pause briefly. Then begin to pass out the bags of dirt. Continue to speak as you do so.)*

That's easy enough to remember, but I want your bag of dirt to remind you of something else, too. I want your bag of dirt to remind you of sin.

Now, sin isn't a nice thing to think about, is it? *(Shake your head and pause briefly for response.)* Of course not! But there is sin in the world. Bad things happen. That's just like dirt. It's here. So is sin.

In fact, we all sin, don't we? Nobody's perfect. Everybody does some kind of bad thing once in a while.

Have you ever told a lie? Have you ever said, "Not me! I didn't do that!" and you really did it? Have you ever been mean to someone? Have you ever disobeyed your parents? None of these things are good, are they? They're all bad things. They're all sins that we all do once in a while.

God doesn't like sin, does he? *(Shake your head and pause for response.)* Of course not! He tells us not to sin, just like an adult says, "Don't get too dirty." But we all sin anyway.

God takes care of our sins, just like we wash dirt away. We'll talk more about that washing next week. But, meanwhile, we have to remind ourselves once in a while that we do get dirty, we do sin.

This time of the year especially, we Christians take a little extra time to remind ourselves of our sins—the bad things we all do. We take extra time to say to God, "We're sorry that we sin. We're sorry that we get dirty again and again."

So, that's really why I gave you that bag of dirt. We're going to take special time this week to tell God that we're sorry for the bad things that we do.

Option

(For specific Lenten use, include the following paragraph.)

Many Christians use the weeks before Easter to think about their sins and tell God that they're sorry for their sins. We often call this time "Lent." You may hear that word often for the next few weeks.

Option

(To address Ash Wednesday, include the following paragraph.)

30

In fact, people often call next (*or* last) Wednesday "Ash Wednesday." They rub ashes on their foreheads to show that they're sorry for their sins. If you hear someone mention Ash Wednesday, you'll know that they too are thinking especially about how sorry they are for their sins.

Continue Lenten Option

Lent lasts for several weeks, so you may hear people say "Lent" or "Lenten" for quite a while yet. Hearing those words is a good reminder to us to tell God that we're sorry for our sins. But we're not going to use our bags of dirt all those weeks. We'll use them just for this one week.

Continue Lesson

This is what I'd like you to do with your bag of dirt: Take it home and put it on a shelf or table near your bed. Don't take the dirt out of the bag. You'll see it when you go to bed tonight. And when you say your prayers, tell God that you're sorry for any bad things that you did today.

All week, keep your bag of dirt near your bed. All week we're going to remember to tell God that we're sorry for the bad things that we do. Your bag of dirt can remind you to do that every night.

There's one more thing you should remember. Take your bag of dirt back to church with you next week. Can you remember that? This week it will remind you of sin, which is dirty and as common as dirt. Bring it back next week for the rest of the story.

7

. . . No More!

Scripture: If we confess our sins, he is faithful and just and will forgive us our sins and purify us from all unrighteousness (1 John 1:9).

Concept: If we confess our sins, God forgives us.

Objects: None. (You may want a few extra bags of dirt for any child who has forgotten his or hers or who did not attend last week's lesson.)

Did you all bring your bags of dirt? *(Pause for response.)* If anyone forgot, I've got a few extra bags here. Who needs a bag of dirt? *(Pass out a bag of dirt to any child who needs one.)*

How many of you remembered to use your bag of dirt this week? *(Pause for response.)*

What did your bag of dirt remind you to do? *(Pause for response and repeat responses.)* That's right. Your bag of dirt was supposed to remind you to confess your sins, to tell God that you were sorry for the bad things that you did this past week.

Last week we said that sin is a lot like dirt. It's very common and dirty.

God doesn't like sin; so we try not to do bad things. But we can't help it. We're not perfect. We all sin—we all do bad things once in a while.

So, this past week, we tried to remember to tell God that we're sorry for our sins. We used our bags of dirt to remind us.

Did you become a little tired of looking at that bag of dirt? *(Hold up a bag and look at it.)* It doesn't feel very good to look at this day after day after day, does it?—especially when it reminds us of the bad things we do. Do you like thinking, every single day, about the bad things that you do? *(Shake your head and pause for response.)* Of course not! None of us like to be reminded of our sins.

We already said that God doesn't like sin. He doesn't like to see it either. So, do you know what God said? He said that if we confess our sins, he'll forgive them. He'll forget about them. He won't look at them day after day after day.

That's like washing dirt off your hands, isn't it? *(Put your hand into a bag of dirt.)* My hand is dirty now, but if I wash it, I can get it clean and forget about the dirt.

God washes away our sins through Jesus. He makes us so clean that he forgets about the dirt. All we have to do is say that we're sorry, and he'll forgive us; he'll make us clean.

Now that we've spent a week remembering our sins and saying that we're sorry for them, it's time to move on. God forgives our sins. He'll take that bag of dirt away. *(Collect the bags of dirt from the children individually. Continue to speak as you do so.)*

When you go home today, look at your shelf or wherever you kept your bag of dirt. It won't be there anymore, will it? It will be gone, just like your sins. Your shelf will look as if it never had a bag of dirt on it.

That's just what you look like to God. He's forgiven your sins; to him, you look as if you've never done anything bad.

So, I have nothing to give you today. *(As you speak, put the bags of dirt out of sight.)* There's nothing that I want you to look at to remember your sins. Because you said that you were sorry, God has forgiven you. You look perfectly clean to him. There's nothing to remember. You're forgiven!

Twigs of Praise

(Palm Sunday)

Scripture: He is the image of the invisible God, the firstborn over all creation (Col. 1:15).

Concept: Jesus is King.

Objects: Small twigs from bushes or trees with leaves attached, at least one for each child. (*Note:* This lesson can be used anytime as written. For Palm Sunday, use option 1.)

Option 1

(Use this paragraph on Palm Sunday.)

Can anyone tell me what special day it is today? *(Pause for response.)* Yes, it's Palm Sunday! Today we celebrate something special that happened to Jesus when he lived on earth.

Option 2

(Use this paragraph on any other day.)

Today I want to tell you a true story. It's about something special that happened to Jesus when he lived on earth.

Continue Lesson

When Jesus was alive here, there was a time when all the people were excited about him. They called him their king, and they wanted to honor him. So they did something very special for him, something that they didn't do very often.

They cut branches from palm trees *(mimic what you say)* and waved them in front of Jesus as he walked past. They shouted, "Blessed is the King of Israel!" as they waved their branches.

The people were very excited. This was a custom they usually did not do. It was saved for a special occasion. In this way they honored Jesus as their king. *(Mimic the waving of branches again.)* Honor to our King!

I thought we would do something similar today. Now, we don't have palm trees around here. We can't cut branches off them and wave them as the Israelites did. But we do have lots of these! *(Show the children the twigs.)* I already cut them off for you. We can wave these! *(Pass out the twigs. Continue to speak as you do so.)*

The idea is to wave something, just as we might wave flags at a parade. Waving the twigs says that we're excited. We're excited that we have such a wonderful king.

Look at your twig for a minute. Who made all twigs? Who made all bushes and trees—even palm trees? *(Pause for response.)* Jesus did! People can't make bushes and trees; only Jesus can do that. Jesus is King! *(Wave a twig high and repeat the last sentence.)*

Who made us and every living thing in the world? Who gave us life? *(Pause for response.)* Of course, Jesus did! Only Jesus can give us life. Only Jesus can give anyone life. *(Hold up a twig and wave it.)* Jesus is King!

Who rules over the whole world he made? Who rules over all people? Who rules over any kings or presidents or prime ministers on earth? *(Pause for response.)* Jesus! Jesus is the true King of everything and everybody. *(Hold up a twig and wave it.)* Jesus is King!

Waving branches was a special way people honored Jesus long ago *(wave a twig as you speak),* and now it's our special way to honor him, too. We don't do this very often, but right now this is our way to honor Jesus our King. Can you do this with me? Let's wave our twigs and honor Jesus. *(Wave your twig and say,)* Jesus is King! Jesus is King!

Who made everything in the world and rules over it all? *(Wave your twig as you pause for response.)* Jesus! Let's honor Jesus together; Jesus is King!

Who made every person in the world and is true King of all? *(Wave your twig and pause for response.)* Jesus! Let's honor Jesus together; Jesus is King!

This is not a common thing to do, is it? *(Wave your twig and pause for response.)* Of course not! We don't wave twigs every day.

But Jesus is not a common King. Jesus can do anything. Jesus is King over the whole world!

So we will do something uncommon for our uncommon King. We'll wave our twigs just as the Israelites waved their palm branches. *(Wave your twig while you say,)* Jesus is King! Jesus is King!

Option 1

(Include this paragraph on Palm Sunday only.)

During the service today you may see people waving real palm branches. Or you may hear people talking and singing about palm branches. When you do, listen very closely. When you see or hear about palm branches, you will also hear the word *king*. That's what we're thinking about today: Jesus is King.

Continue Lesson

Long ago, people used palm branches to honor King Jesus. They used palms only because those branches were handy. The point was to honor Jesus as King. We're using these twigs instead of palms. The point is to honor Jesus as King.

Have you ever used a twig to honor Jesus as King? *(Shake your head and pause for response.)* Probably not! But you did today. You did something special to honor Jesus as King.

Take your twig home. Put it someplace where you'll see it this week. Every time you see it, remember what we did here today. We honored Jesus as our King. Every time you see your twig, remember to say, "Jesus is King!"

9

Everyday Service

(Maundy Thursday)

Scripture: Now that I, your Lord and Teacher, have washed your feet, you also should wash one another's feet. I have set you an example that you should do as I have done for you (John 13:14–15).

Serve wholeheartedly, as if you were serving the Lord, not men (Eph. 6:7).

Concept: Christians should be willing to perform humble service.

Object: A towel in a paper bag. (*Note:* This lesson can be used anytime as written. The option for specific Maundy Thursday use is included on page 41.)

Today I brought along something that's very common. Each of you has used one of these, probably today. You use one of these often, but you don't think about it often. It's a common thing that you find in your house. Can you guess what it is? *(Pause for response. Repeat responses.)*

Let's stop guessing; I'll show you what it is. It's . . . a *(slowly take the towel out of the bag)* . . . towel!

What do we use towels for? *(Pause for response. Repeat responses.)* We use towels to dry our hands after we wash them. We even use small towels to wash ourselves. We use small towels to wash dishes and larger towels to dry dishes. We use towels to clean up spills. We use towels for all sorts of everyday chores.

Yet, we hardly ever think about towels, and we don't think they're special. Have you ever wanted a towel as a gift? *(Shake your head and pause for response.)* No, you'd probably much rather receive a toy or even some clothes. When visitors come to your house, does Mom or Dad set towels around where everyone can see them? *(Shake your head and pause for response.)* Of course not; towels usually just hang on a hook somewhere.

Towels are humble, everyday objects that we don't think about often. Yet, we need them all the time for everyday chores.

I'm sure that Jesus used towels when he was on earth. In fact, there's a story in the Bible about Jesus using a towel. The story tells how Jesus washed his disciples' feet. What do you think he used to dry his disciples' feet? *(Pause for response.)* Sure, he used a towel. Maybe it was a lot like this one. *(Hold up the towel. Keep it up.)*

Of course, that story isn't really about using a towel. Jesus wanted to teach his disciples a lesson when he used that towel. *(Put the towel down.)* After he washed his disciples' feet, he said that they should do the same for each other. He wanted his disciples to help each other, to serve each other.

Option

(Include the following paragraphs for Maundy Thursday or adjust for use anytime during Lent.)

In fact, do you know *when* Jesus washed his disciples' feet and told them to serve each other? *(Pause slightly.)* The night before he died!

Can anyone tell me what day it will be tomorrow? *(Pause for response.)* That's right, tomorrow will be Good Friday, the anniversary of Jesus' death. So tonight, we remember that night before Jesus died. That's when he told his disciples to serve each other. That's also when he washed his disciples' feet.

Option

(Include this if you have a foot-washing ceremony.)

To remember what Jesus did for his disciples the night before he died, we're going to do the same thing. If you watch closely tonight, you'll see some people washing other people's feet. That's the adults' reminder to serve each other as Jesus served.

Continue Lesson

Would you like to wash someone's dirty feet? *(Grimace and pause for response.)* No! Washing your feet is an everyday chore, but it's a humble chore. There's not much honor in it. It's just something that must be done. If you wash someone else's feet, you're doing a humble service.

That's the lesson that Jesus taught. Jesus told his disciples that they should do humble service for each other. God tells us elsewhere in the Bible that we should serve each other and we should serve humbly.

God says that we should be willing to do things for others without getting attention for it. We should help each other with everyday chores.

Can you think of ways we can help each other? What are some humble, everyday things we can do? *(Pause for response. Repeat responses. You may have to prompt the children with questions.)* Can we help around the house? Can we help set up chairs for Sunday school? Can we help a friend with his or her chores?

Now we've got some ideas. Jesus wants us to help each other with humble, everyday service. We won't get much honor for it. We'll just be very helpful— just like this towel. *(Hold up the towel and keep it up.)* Nobody thinks about it much, but everyone uses it. I brought it along so that we could think about it and about humble service for a little while.

The next time you use a towel, look at the towel and think about it for a minute. It can remind you of Jesus washing his disciples' feet. It can remind you that Jesus wants us all to be his towels and serve each other humbly.

10

A Reminder

(Lord's Supper)

MEMORY VERSE:

Scripture: Do this in remembrance of me (Luke 22:19).

Concept: Remember Jesus.

Object: A loaf of bread. A glass is optional. (*Note:* This lesson can be used anytime as written. The option for specific Lord's Supper use is included at the end of the lesson.)

Today we're going to talk about two of the most important things in the whole wide world. I hope you remember them for a long, long time.

First is one of the most important things in the whole wide world that you need to keep you alive. Can you think of something that you absolutely need to live? *(Don't pause here.)*

How about toys? Are toys the most important thing in the world? Will you die without toys? *(Shake your head and pause for response.)* No! Toys are not that important. They're nice to have, but you won't die without them. Toys are not one of the most important things in the world.

Do you absolutely need clothes? Will you die if you don't wear shoes? *(Shake your head and pause for response.)* Of course you won't. How about a hat? Do you absolutely need a hat to live? *(Shake your head and pause for response.)* No! A hat may be important at times, but it's not one of the most important things in the world. You won't die without a hat. In fact, clothes are important but are not one of the most important things in the whole world.

How about food? Do you absolutely need food to live? Will you die if you don't have food? *(Nod your head and pause for response.)* Yes! Food is one of the most important things in the world to us. We need food to keep us alive. If we don't have food, we'll die.

I brought along some very common food *(display the loaf of bread)*—a loaf of bread. Everyone eats bread at times. *(Take out one slice of bread as you speak.)* We eat other foods, too, but bread is very common. *(Hold up the slice of bread.)* Is this familiar to all of you? *(Nod your head and pause for response.)* Of course, you've all eaten bread. This bread stands for food, one of the most important things in the world.

Option

(If you use a glass, use this paragraph.)

We must both eat and drink. We die if we don't get enough water with our food. *(Display the glass.)* So this glass stands for a drink. *(Hold up the bread and the glass.)* These things stand for food and drink, which we must have to stay alive.

Continue Lesson

What happens when you don't eat? How do you feel? *(Pause for response.)* Hungry! That's right, you become hungry if you go without food for very long. Being hungry is a reminder to eat. *(Hold up the loaf of bread.)*

So, we never forget to eat, do we? We may forget for a little while, but pretty soon our stomachs remind us that we absolutely need food. *(Hold up the loaf of bread.)*

Option

(If you use the glass, include the next two paragraphs.)

What happens when you don't drink for a while? How do you feel? *(Pause for response.)* Thirsty! That's right, you become thirsty if you go without something to drink for very long. Being thirsty is a reminder to drink. *(Hold up the glass.)*

So, we never forget to drink, do we? We may forget for a little while, but pretty soon we're thirsty, and that thirstiness reminds us to drink. *(Hold up the bread with the glass.)* We always have reminders to eat and drink.

Continue Lesson

Food is one of the most important things in the world to us. We absolutely need it or we'll die. But we don't forget to eat, do we? We become hungry, and that reminds us of how important food is to us.

Now let's talk about another very important thing. It isn't like food, but it's also very, very important. Or, rather, *he* is very, very important.

Who is the most important person who ever lived? He's more important to us than anybody else in the whole wide world. He's more important than Mom or Dad or anybody else you can think of. Who is that? Who's the most important person who ever lived? *(Pause for response.)* Jesus! Of course.

Jesus is the only person who can save us from our sins. If Jesus didn't live, we wouldn't be Christians. If Jesus didn't live, our souls would die. Jesus came to save us forever. Because Jesus lived, we can live in heaven with him. Without Jesus, we're lost. Jesus is the most important person who ever lived, now and forever.

Without food, we die. Without Jesus, our souls die. *(Hold up the bread.)* Food is absolutely necessary to keep our bodies alive. Jesus is absolutely necessary to give us life in heaven.

Our bodies automatically remind us to eat some food. Do our hearts automatically remind us to think about Jesus? *(Shake your head and pause for response.)* No, not really. Our hearts (*or* souls) aren't that good. Our hearts (*or* souls) don't automatically become hungry for Jesus. Sometimes we forget about him. We can go for days without thinking about Jesus.

So, because our hearts (*or* souls) aren't that good, we need a reminder. We should have something that reminds us to think about Jesus and stay close to him.

Here's your reminder! *(Hold up the loaf of bread, then take out one slice and hold that up.)* Do you think that you're going to eat bread this week? *(Nod and pause for response.)* Probably. Most people eat bread every day.

This week, we're going to have the bread remind us of Jesus. We need food to live; we need Jesus for eternal life. Every time that you eat a slice of bread this week, think about Jesus. Can you do that? *(Nod your head and pause for response.)*

When you eat a slice of bread *(hold up the bread)* think, "This should remind me of Jesus." Then ask Jesus to help you stay close to him.

It's too bad that our hearts don't automatically remember to stay close to Jesus, but they don't. So, we'll try to remind ourselves with this food. *(Hold up the bread.)* We need food for our bodies. We need Jesus in our hearts. This week, remember Jesus.

Option

(Add the following paragraph if you use the lesson at a Lord's Supper celebration.)

Do you know what? Children aren't the only people who forget Jesus. Adults need a reminder, too. In fact, Jesus knew that we would need a reminder. So Jesus told us to use bread and wine to remind us of him. Pretty soon, you'll see adults pass *(or* come to the front for) some bread and some wine *(or* grape juice). That bread and wine *(or* juice) are the adults' reminder of Jesus and that he saves us from sin. Their reminder is a lot like your reminder this week. So, when you see the adults pass *(or* come up for) the bread and when you eat your bread this week, you can remember that we all need Jesus. This week, remember Jesus.

11

The Shape of Salvation

(Good Friday)

Scripture: He forgave us all our sins, having canceled the written code, with its regulations, that was against us and that stood opposed to us; he took it away, nailing it to the cross (Col. 2:13–14).

Concept: Jesus died on a cross for our sins.

Objects: Four paper shapes: one star, one circle, one square or rectangle, and one cross. (*Note:* This lesson can be used anytime as written. The option for specific Good Friday use is included near the end of the lesson.)

Let's look at some shapes today. There are shapes all around us. *(Indicate the walls, the doors, the windows.)* What shape is that wall? *(Point to a wall.)* Is it a square? *(Pause for response.)* That's right, it's quite close to square *(or rectangle, if mentioned).*

(Point to the clock.) What shape is the clock? *(Pause for response.)* Yes, it's round.

(Pick out a few more shapes that are quite obvious—the round top of a water glass, the rectangle shape of a Bible, the shape of a button, etc. Finish by making a few shapes with your fingers.)

48

Sometimes shapes can remind us of certain things. *(Show the children the star.)* What is this? *(Pause for response.)* Of course, a star. This can remind you of any star, even the Christmas star. Sometimes we use stars to show that someone's work is really good. The shape of a star can remind us of many things.

What does this shape remind you of? *(Hold up the circle and pause for response. Repeat responses.)* Yes! We've seen circles already. So this circle can remind us of the clock or the glass, or maybe even a balloon or a ball. A circle like this can remind us of many things.

What does this shape remind you of? *(Hold up the square or the rectangle and pause for response. Repeat responses.)* Sure, this can remind you of a box, a wall, a book, even the Bible. We see squares all around us, so a square can remind us of many different things.

What about this shape? What does this remind you of? *(Hold up the cross and pause for response.)* That's right, this reminds us of the cross on which Jesus died.

Can you see any crosses here in church? *(Pause for response. If there are no crosses within view, ask the children if they can remember where in the church they can see a cross.)* Christians often use the shape of a cross to remind themselves and to tell others that Jesus died on a cross for our sins.

Does this shape remind you of anything else? *(Hold up the paper cross shape again and pause for response.)* I don't think so. This cross shape says, loudly and clearly to everyone, Jesus died on a cross for our sins. This shape reminds us only of Jesus.

Option

(If you use this lesson on Good Friday, include the following paragraphs.)

Today is a very special day. Today we especially remember the day that Jesus was crucified—killed on a cross—for our sins.

Jesus died for us on a Friday. We call today Good Friday because Jesus took away our sins when he died on the cross that Friday.

We know that Jesus' death isn't the end of the story. We'll celebrate Easter in two days but today we especially remember the cross of Jesus.

Continue Lesson

These other shapes can remind you of all sorts of things: *(hold up the square or the rectangle)* books, doors, walls, boxes; *(hold up the circle)* clocks, balls, balloons; *(hold up the star)* real stars, stars meaning good work. But this shape *(hold up the cross)* reminds us of one thing: Jesus died on a cross for our sins.

I'd like you to look at different shapes today. See how many square shapes you can find and how many round shapes. You may even want to look for stars. Don't try to count all those shapes. The world is full of shapes. But while you're thinking about shapes today, look for crosses. See how many crosses you can find. And each time you see a cross, think about the real cross. Jesus died on the cross to save us from our sins.

12

The Message of Easter

(Easter)

Scripture: For what I received I passed on to you as of first importance: that Christ died for our sins according to the Scriptures, that he was buried, that he was raised on the third day according to the Scriptures (1 Cor. 15:3).

Concept: Although Jesus died, he lives!

Objects: Several symbols of Easter. Use whatever is most common in your area. An Easter egg and a bunny are used for demonstration here. (*Note:* This lesson can be used on Easter or at any time after Ash Wednesday.)

I've brought some things that are supposed to remind us of Easter. Let's take a look at them.

How many of you have seen one of these? (*Show the children an Easter egg and pause for response.*) Of course, we all see different kinds of eggs this time of year. They're in stores, and people use them for decoration. Some people love to dye eggs around Easter. Eggs are very common right now. They're used to celebrate Easter.

Can anyone tell me *why* we have eggs at Easter? *(Appear puzzled and pause slightly for response.)* I don't know. Some people say that an egg reminds us of new life. Maybe an egg is supposed to remind us of spring somehow. I don't know why an egg stands for Easter. But, we call these colored eggs Easter eggs. So now, colored eggs remind us of Easter.

How many of you have seen one of these? *(Hold up a picture of an Easter bunny and pause for response.)* Of course, we all see pictures of bunnies this time of year. Sometimes we see stuffed bunnies, or we may even see real bunnies. Bunnies are very common right now. They're supposed to remind us of Easter.

Can anyone tell me *why* bunnies are supposed to remind us of Easter? *(Appear puzzled and pause slightly for response.)* I don't know. Some people say that bunnies come out in the spring. Some people pretend that a bunny brings Easter eggs. We call those bunnies Easter bunnies. So now, bunnies remind us of Easter.

(Continue in this manner with each Easter symbol. Ask how many have seen it. Comment on how common it is this time of the year. Ask why it's supposed to remind us of Easter. Mention a few possibilities. Finish with the comment that each has become a symbol of Easter.)

So, all these things remind us of Easter *(show each symbol as you mention it):* an Easter egg, a bunny . . . (a chick, an Easter basket, *etc.*) They remind us of Easter.

Now we're going to put all of these reminders away *(place items behind you)* to talk about the real thing—Easter! Why should we remember Easter? What happened on the very first Easter day long, long ago? *(Pause for response. If it's not forthcoming, prompt the children with the question,* Who rose from the dead?) That's right! Jesus rose from the dead on the first Easter.

Jesus died on a cross. We talked about his death (*or* celebrated that) last Friday. After Jesus died, his friends buried him, just as we bury dead people today. But that next Sunday, Jesus rose from the dead! He made himself alive and walked right out of his grave. That's what we celebrate today (*if it's Easter, say,* on Easter Sunday). That's what Easter's all about.

All by himself, Jesus became alive again. Because Jesus is God he could raise himself and prove that no one can kill God. Jesus was stronger than death. That's why Easter is such a happy celebration. Jesus rose from the dead!

Jesus is alive today, and he has power over everything, even death! Your Lord, who loves you, is alive and real and rules over everything.

Now, isn't that good reason for joy? That's why we celebrate Easter.

So, these reminders *(set the symbols in front of you again)* don't mean much unless you have the whole story. An Easter egg, a bunny *(hold up each symbol as you mention it)* will probably always remind you of Easter. But now, whenever you see one of these reminders, think of Easter and *then* think about the real story of Easter: Jesus rose from the dead! Jesus is truly alive!

13

Flowering for God

Scripture: But grow in the grace and knowledge of our Lord and Savior Jesus Christ (2 Peter 3:18).

Concept: We should try to grow as Christians.

Objects: A flower bud and an open flower, both on their stalks.

This time of year we see lots of *(hold up the flower bud)* buds! Lots of plants seemed to rest over the winter, but now they're waking up. Grass is turning green, trees have buds, and all different plants have buds. When you go home today, look around your yard and see how many *(hold up the flower bud and keep it up)* buds you can see.

This isn't going to remain a bud forever, is it? What do you think this bud is going to become? *(Pause for response. As you wait, put the bud down slowly and hold up the flower.)* Yes, it's going to become a flower! At least, we hope it will flower.

Yet, this bud *(hold up the bud)* needs a little care, a little tending, to open into a flower. Usually God sends the right weather to make buds into flowers. If we have buds like this in the house, we must tend them to be sure they flower.

Who can tell me what I should do with this bud to make sure it opens into a flower? Can I put it down like this *(put the bud on the floor),* or should I give it some water? *(Pause for response.)* Of course, it needs water to stay alive and become a flower. I should put it in a glass of water.

If I put this in some water and then into a dark closet, would it bloom? *(Pause for response.)* Should I put it in sunlight? *(Pause for response.)* Of course, this bud needs water and light to open. I'll have to put it in the light.

So, I should take care of this bud if I want it to become a flower, shouldn't I? I should give it water and sunlight. If I tend this bud it will become a *(hold up the flower)* beautiful flower. But if I don't take care of it, it will probably never open. It will just wither and die.

I brought this bud and flower along today because they remind me of Christians. In a way, we Christians *(indicate the children with a sweep of your arm)* resemble this bud. *(Hold up the bud.)* We can grow into beautiful Christians, flowers for God *(hold up the flower),* but we need tending. We have to do certain things to make sure that we'll grow.

What do you think we must do to be sure that we grow into flowering Christians? *(Pause for response. Repeat responses. You may have to prompt the children with questions.)* Should we listen to stories of Jesus and read our Bibles? Should we pray to Jesus to help us stay close to him as we grow? Should we try to do the things that Jesus wants us to do? Should we try to show God's love to people? Those are all good things that we can do to grow as Christians.

There are two things we should do that are especially important. We should always pray to Jesus to keep us close to him. And we should read or listen to our Bibles so that we know what God wants us to do.

Doing those things is just like giving this bud *(hold up the bud)* water and sunlight. If we don't give this bud water and sunlight, it will wither and die. If we don't read or listen to our Bibles and pray, we will wither and die as Christians.

But if we do tend this bud carefully, it will become a *(hold up the flower)* beautiful flower. And if we tend our lives to stay close to God, we can become beautiful Christian flowers for him.

14

Handle with Care!

(Earth Day)

Scripture: The earth is the LORD's, and everything in it, the world, and all who live in it (Ps. 24:1).

Concept: The earth and everything in it belongs to God; we should handle it with care.

Objects: At least five pictures of natural objects, both animate and inanimate. (*Note:* This lesson can be used anytime as written. For Earth Day, use option.)

Option

(If you are observing Earth Day, begin here.)

This week we're going to celebrate a special day. It's called Earth Day. If you listen carefully to people talk this week, you may hear them mention things like air and soil and trees and animals. That's because they're thinking especially about the earth and everything in it.

Lesson

(If you are not observing Earth Day, begin here.)

I wanted to bring the whole world inside today to show you, but I couldn't do that, so I brought some pictures instead. These are just a few of the things we find in the world.

Can anyone tell me what this is? *(Show the children a picture and pause for response.)* Yes, it's a bird *(or whatever)!*

Who made this bird? Who makes all birds? *(Pause for response.)* Of course, God did! We all know that. God made all birds.

Whose bird is this? If God made it, does it belong to him? *(Pause for response.)* Yes, this is God's bird. All birds belong to God. He made them, and they are his.

Can we enjoy God's birds? Can we listen to birds sing? Can we put out bird feeders and watch birds? *(Pause for response.)* Yes, we can! Lots of people love to watch birds and listen to them sing. I think that God wants us to enjoy his birds.

Can we do anything that we want to do to God's birds? Can we pull out their feathers, or tie their beaks shut, or do mean things to them? *(Shake your head and pause for response.)* No, I don't think we should. They're God's birds, not ours. We can enjoy them, but we should handle them with care.

(Proceed in this manner with all your pictures. Show the picture and ask what it is. Ask who made it. Ask who owns it. Ask if we may use [or enjoy] it. Ask if we can do anything we want with it. Finish with the statement that we can enjoy [or use] it, but we should handle it with care.)

We've been looking at lots of pictures only because I can't bring all of these things inside to show you. But you can see them whenever you go outside.

(If the children can see out a nearby window, direct their attention to the window and repeat the above formula with at least one item they can see through the window.)

I think you get the idea, don't you? God made the earth and everything in it. It all belongs to him. We may use it and enjoy it, but we should handle it with care.

This week I'd like you to try a little exercise. Every time that you go outside, pick something up—maybe a stick or a stone, a bud or a flower, maybe even a little bug—or pretend that you're picking up a bird. Pick something up as soon as you go outside. Look at what you've picked up and say, "God made this stick (*or* stone *or* flower *or* bird). It's his. I may enjoy it. I should handle it with care." It's God's world; handle it with care.

15

Let's Sing!

Scripture: Come, let us sing for joy to the Lord; let us shout aloud to the Rock of our salvation (Ps. 95:1).

Concept: We can sing God's praises.

Object: A bird song. If you can make a bird call, do so. If you know someone who can and is willing to help, use him or her. You can also use a recording of bird calls or a mechanical bird call. The children should hear a bird call at certain times.

 B e very quiet for a few minutes. I want you to hear something. *(Play the bird call for several seconds.)* What was that? *(Pause for response.)* Of course, that was a bird call.

This is as close as I can come to a real bird call. *(Show the children the gadget, recorder, or however you reproduced the bird call.)* I've heard many bird calls outside lately, but I brought this with me to make sure that you heard some kind of bird song.

Have any of you noticed the birds singing outside lately? Take some time this week to listen to the birds sing. You should sit outside very quietly. Just listen for a while, and you'll hear bird songs. Birds are singing all around us.

They sing often and loudly this time of the year. They sing when the sun rises. They sing before the sun sets. They sing to their mates. They sing to claim territories. They sing for the joy of being alive on a wonderful spring day. They sing praises to God.

The Bible says that everything that has life and breath should praise the Lord. This time of the year, the birds are singing their praises to him.

Do you blame them? It's such a wonderful time of year, isn't it? *(Nod and pause for response.)* The weather's becoming warmer, the sun is out, the grass is green, and flowers are beginning to bloom. The whole world seems to be singing God's praises. The birds are just a part of it.

This is a fine time for us to sing God's praises, too. The Bible tells us to sing God's praises. This time of year makes many people want to sing. This is a good time to sing God's praises.

Option 1

(If you want the children to sing during the lesson, use this paragraph.)

Why don't we sing a song together? How about "Jesus Loves Me" *(or a song the children know and love to sing)? (Do as many songs as time allows.)*

Option 2

(If you do not want to sing during the lesson, use this paragraph.)

When you go back to your seats, we'll all sing together. That singing could be just a beginning. You can sing all week, aloud or to yourself, alone or with other people. God likes us to sing praises to him. This week would be a fine week for singing.

Continue Lesson

Let's do some extra singing this week. Listen to the birds sing; their songs praise God. Then add your songs. Take some time to sing God's praises.

16

Keep in Touch

(Prayer Day)

MEMORY VERSE

Scripture: Pray continually (1 Thess. 5:17).

Concept: We can talk to God anytime and anywhere.

Object: A cellular telephone. (*Note:* This lesson can be used anytime as written. The option for use on Prayer Day is included near the end of the lesson.)

I've got a gadget here that's been very, very useful. (*Hold up the phone.*) Can anyone tell me what it is? (*Pause for response. Repeat responses. You may have to prompt the children with questions.*) Yes, it's a telephone; but it's a special type of telephone. Is it connected to a cord? Must I plug this phone in? Must I use this phone in the house or in a certain area? Does anyone know exactly what this phone is called?

Well, it's called a cellular phone, but the name isn't really important. What's really important about this phone is that I can use it anytime, anywhere.

Some people use phones like this in their cars. Have you ever seen someone sitting in a car talking on a telephone? (*Pause for response.*) Yes, I've seen that once in a while. This is the kind of phone people use in cars. *(Hold up the phone.)* When you're riding in your car, especially if you're on a busy highway, look at people in other cars. You may see someone using a phone like this.

You can use this phone anywhere. If you're at school and want to call home, just take out the phone *(mimic your words)* and call home. If you're playing at a friend's house and want to call home, just take out the phone *(mimic your words)* and call. If you're at the park, or the beach, or a ball game, or the mall—wherever you are—if you want to talk to someone, just take out the phone *(mimic your words)* and call the person.

Not very many of us own phones like this yet. *(If the phone isn't yours, say,* In fact, I borrowed this phone to show you.*)* How many of you have a phone like this, a phone that you can use anywhere, anytime? *(Pause for response.)* I thought so; lots of people don't own these. Most of us can't call someone anytime and anywhere we please.

That's no problem. There is one person whom you and I *can* call anytime and anywhere. We don't even need a phone like this to do it. This person wants to hear from us. Whom can we talk to anytime and anywhere? *(Pause for response.)* Of course, God (*or,* Jesus)! We can talk to God anytime, all the time, anywhere, everywhere.

How can we talk to God? *(Pause for response. Assume a position of prayer if the answer isn't forthcoming.)* We can pray! Prayer is talking to God.

Sometimes we don't close our eyes and fold our hands to pray. Sometimes we don't pray aloud. We just talk to Jesus in our hearts. That's praying.

Do we have to be home or in church to pray? *(Pause for response.)* No. We can pray in our cars, at a friend's house, at school, at the park, at the beach, at a ball game, at the mall. We can pray wherever we are.

Do we have to wait for a meal or before we go to bed to pray? *(Pause for response.)* Of course not! We can talk to God anytime. God will always hear us when we pray. God doesn't wait for certain times of the day. Anytime we want to, we can talk to him.

In fact, the Bible tells us that we should pray continually. Praying continually means that we should always be talking to God. Many times every day we can say a little prayer and talk to God. It doesn't matter where we are or what time of day it is.

We don't even need a gadget like this. *(Hold up the cellular phone.)* This is nice for talking to people anytime and anywhere. But when we talk to God, all we need to do is talk to him in our hearts.

Option

(Include the following paragraph if you use the lesson on or near Prayer Day.)

Sometimes we have special days on which we all get together to pray. That's what we're doing today. *(Or if it isn't Prayer Day yet, say,* That's what we'll do on Prayer Day.) It's sort of like a conference call on the telephone *(mimic using the phone):* Everybody gets together to talk to God. Then we pray together about things that we all think about. That's a special time to share our prayer.

Continue Lesson

(Hold up the phone.) You probably won't see someone using a phone like this every day; but pay special attention when you do see it. Just as someone talks on this phone anytime, anyplace, you can talk to God anytime, anyplace.

17

Children of God

(Mother's Day)

Scripture: How great is the love the Father has lavished on us, that we should be called children of God! (1 John 3:1).

Concept: God is our ultimate caregiver.

Object: None to take with you. (*Note:* This lesson can be used anytime as written. For Mother's Day, use option.)

Option

(Begin here if you use this lesson on Mother's Day.)

Can anyone tell me what day it is today? *(Pause for response.)* Yes, you may have heard by now that today is Mother's Day. We take special time today to honor our mothers and say thank you for everything that they do for us.

(Note: This paragraph is optional.) Let's have our mothers stand up for a minute, so that we can see them. *(Turn to the congregation.)* Will the mothers of these children please stand up? *(Turn back to the children.)* Can you find your mother? You may wave if you want to. *(Pause very briefly, then turn to the congregation.)* You may sit down; thank you. *(Turn back to the children.)*

Lesson

(Begin here if you do not use this lesson on Mother's Day.)

Today we're going to talk about parents, both mothers and fathers. We're going to start with mothers. How many of you have a mother living at your house? *(Pause for response.)* Not all families have mothers, but many do.

What does your mother do? *(Pause for response. Repeat the children's responses. Prompt them with questions to include all activities. Turn their attention toward care-giving activities.)* Does your mother fix meals? Does she take care of your clothes? Does she make your house into a warm, loving home? Does she take care of you? Does she go to work every day? Does she help buy your food and clothes?

Some families don't have mothers. *(If children without mothers are present, direct your questions toward them. Pause for response after each question.)* Then, who fixes the meals? Who takes care of your clothes? Who buys your food and clothes? Who takes care of you?

Is there anyone here who has to cook his own meals and buy her own clothes? *(Shake your head and pause briefly for response.)* Of course not! You all have parents or some adult to take care of you.

Who, do you think, gave you your mother and father (*or* the adults who care for you)? Who makes sure that someone will take care of you? *(Pause for response.)* Yes, God!

God gave you parents (*or* adults) to take care of you. God knows that children can't take care of themselves. So he gave you parents (*or* adults) to care for you. God makes sure that your parents (*or* adults in your house) will have enough food for you and enough clothes to keep you warm. So, God takes care of you through your parents (*or* the adults in your house.)

Why does God take such good care of you? *(Pause briefly for response.)* That's right, because he loves you. The Bible says that God loves you so much he calls you his child. And, since you are his child, he takes wonderful care of you.

He takes care of you by giving you mothers and fathers or just mothers or just fathers or other adults who love you and care for you. Behind every adult who cares for you is God, who calls you his child.

So today we want to honor our parents and the adults who take care of us. (*Option:* Today we want to pay special honor to our mothers.) When you go home, thank them (*or* her) for loving you and taking care of you.

Then thank God for giving you your mother (*or* parents *or* adults in your house.) And thank God especially for loving you, taking such good care of you, and making you his beloved child.

18

Jesus Doesn't Live Here

(Ascension Day)

Scripture: This same Jesus, who has been taken from you into heaven, will come back in the same way you have seen him go into heaven (Acts 1:11).

Concept: Jesus lives in heaven but will return to earth.

Objects: A personal letter in its envelope, a Bible. (*Note:* This lesson can be used anytime as written. The option for specific Ascension Day use is included near the end of the lesson.)

I received a nice letter this week. *(Hold up the letter in the envelope.)* It's from my sister *(or some relative or friend who lives out of town)*. She doesn't live here in (your city or area). She lives far away in (another city, state, or country).

Since she lives so far away, she sends letters to keep in touch. *(Hold up the letter.)* In this letter she tells me that she's fine, and she tells me about what she's doing right now.

How many of you have grandmas and grandpas or other friends or relatives who live far away? *(Pause for response. Ask a few children exactly who it is that lives far away and where they live. Repeat the children's responses, naming the names the children use, to make the distant person real. Finish with a comment about how far away _____ lives.)*

Most of us have at least one person we love who lives far, far away. In fact, I know of a certain very special person who loves you and who lives very far away right now. Can you think of who that special person is? *(Pause for response. You may have to prompt the children with questions.)* Who lived on earth once but now lives in heaven? Didn't Jesus say that he loves his children? Yes! Jesus loves you very much, but he lives far away in heaven.

Although we can't see him, we know that Jesus is alive—just like Grandma and Grandpa, or my sister. He just lives far, far away in heaven. That's farther than where Grandma and Grandpa live. That's farther than where my sister lives. *(Hold up the letter as you speak.)*

Of course, we can read news of Jesus, just as I read this letter from my sister or as you read letters from Grandma and Grandpa. Where can we read stories of Jesus? *(Pause for response as you hold up the Bible.)* Of course, we can read about Jesus in the Bible. So, although he lives far away right now, we can keep in touch by reading and listening to Bible stories about him. That's like Jesus' letter to us. *(Hold up the letter again.)*

In fact, I received some very good news in this letter from my sister. *(Take the letter out of the envelope as you speak.)* She says that she's coming to (your city or area). She doesn't say exactly when, but she is coming!

Do your grandmas and grandpas come to (your city or area) sometimes? *(Pause slightly for response.)* Do you think that they are coming here again? *(Nod and pause for response.)* Maybe you don't know exactly when, but they'll probably come back. Some day your family might get a letter like this *(hold up the letter)* that says, "We're coming to (your city or area)!"

We already have a letter from Jesus saying that he's coming back! *(Hold up the Bible.)* Before Jesus left for heaven, he promised that he'd come back to earth. *(Note: Include the next sentence only if you do not mention Ascension Day.)* And, the very day that he left, an angel said to his disciples, *(open the Bible and read Acts 1:11).*

Option

(If you give this lesson on Ascension Day, include the following paragraphs.)

Today we celebrate the day that Jesus went to heaven. We read about that day in the Bible. The Bible says, *(read Luke 24:50–51).* Jesus went to heaven!

But the Bible also says that Jesus is coming back. It says, *(read Acts 1:10–11).* The Bible *(hold up the Bible for all to see)* says that Jesus, who lives in heaven now, will come back to earth.

Continue Lesson

That news is just like the news in this letter I got from my sister *(hold up the letter),* only better yet.

Jesus, who lives so far away in heaven, is definitely coming back to us! He promised! We don't know when, but he's going to come.

Meanwhile, we'll just have to keep reading letters about him *(hold up the Bible)* to know what he did and what he's doing. And every time a letter like this *(hold up the letter)* comes from someone we love, it can remind us of Jesus, who lives far away in heaven but has said that he is coming back.

19

The Holy Spirit

(Pentecost)

Scripture: The wind blows wherever it pleases. You hear its sound, but you cannot tell where it comes from or where it is going. So it is with everyone born of the Spirit (John 3:8).

Concept: We can see and feel the work of the invisible Holy Spirit.

Object: A deflated balloon. Optional: a balloon for each child. (*Note:* This lesson can be used anytime as written. For Pentecost, use option at the beginning.)

Option

(Begin here for use on Pentecost.)

Can anyone tell me what special day it is? *(Hold up deflated balloon and pause for response.)* This is a day that not many people know about. It's called Pentecost.

The name of the day isn't really important. But what we celebrate is very important. Today we celebrate the coming of the Holy Spirit into the world.

The Holy Spirit is very very difficult to imagine because we can't see and touch a spirit. So we're going to talk about something that you can see and touch, first. Maybe that thing can help you think about the Holy Spirit.

Lesson

(Begin here for use on any other day.)

Is there anything in this balloon? *(Hold up deflated balloon and pause for response.)* No! It's just a little, limp balloon.

(Blow up the balloon and show it to the children.) Is there anything in this balloon now? *(Pause for response.)* Of course, there's air in the balloon. You saw me blow the balloon up.

Now watch closely for the air to come out. *(Hold the balloon up for the children to see, and gradually release the air.)* Can you see the air come out of the balloon? *(Pause for response.)* Of course not.

Can you see air? *(Shake your head as you ask, and pause for response.)* No! No one can see air. We say that air is *invisible.* Although air is real and all around us *(indicate with your hands),* we can't see it. It's invisible.

We can't see air, but we know that it's here, don't we? *(Blow up the balloon and show it to the children.)* How do you know that there is air in this balloon? *(Pause for response. You may have to help them by asking,* Can you see what the air does to the balloon?*)* You can see that the balloon is blown up; it's filled with air. You can see what air does to the balloon. Although air is invisible, you can see its work on the balloon.

Blow a little bit of air over your hand. *(Blow over the back of your hand to demonstrate.)* Can you feel the air blowing over your hand? *(Pause for response.)* Of course you can! Can you see the air you blow? *(Pause for response.)* Of course not!

Air is invisible, but you can feel what it does. You can feel its work, and you can see its work. *(Hold up the inflated balloon.)*

The Holy Spirit is like air—invisible, but you can see and feel his work. The Holy Spirit is God, and the Bible tells us that the Spirit works just like wind; you can't see the Spirit, but you can see what the Spirit does, and you can feel *(put your hand over your heart)* the Spirit's work.

When you listen to Bible stories and feel love in your heart *(put your hand over your heart)* for Jesus, that's the Holy Spirit working. The Holy Spirit put that love in your heart.

When a person who doesn't love Jesus changes and becomes a Christian, who worked in that person's heart? *(Pause for response.)* Yes, the Holy Spirit!

When someone shows that they love Jesus, you can *see* the work of the Holy Spirit. When you feel love for Jesus in your heart, you're *feeling* the work of the Holy Spirit.

You'll never see the Holy Spirit on earth, because he's invisible, just like the wind. But you'll feel and see the work of the Spirit, because he's God, and he's right here working among us.

Although we're talking especially about the Spirit today, we often tend to forget about him. That's why

I brought this balloon. *(Hold up the balloon, then inflate it.)* Balloons can help you remember the Holy Spirit, especially when they're blown up. Just like the air in this balloon, the Holy Spirit is invisible, but you can see and feel his work. *(Let the air out slowly over your hand.)*

Option

(If you have brought balloons for the children, add this paragraph.)

To help you think about the Holy Spirit this week, I've brought a balloon for each of you. Before you go to bed tonight, blow up your balloon and tie it. *(Blow up the balloon and tie it to keep the air inside.)* Then think of the Holy Spirit, who's invisible—just like the air—but who you can feel working in your heart. When you wake up tomorrow morning, see if your balloon still has air in it. Then think once more of the Holy Spirit, who's invisible, but whose work you can see in people who love Jesus.

20

Our Heavenly Father

(Father's Day)

> **Scripture:** I will be a Father to you, and you will be my sons and daughters, says the Lord Almighty (2 Cor. 6:18).
>
> **Concept:** We should obey God, our loving Father.
>
> **Object:** None to take with you. (*Note:* This lesson can be used anytime as written. For Father's Day, use option.)

Option

(Begin here if you use this lesson on Father's Day.)

Can anyone tell me what day it is today? *(Pause for response.)* Yes, you may have heard by now that today is Father's Day. We take special time today to honor our fathers and say thank you for everything that they do for us.

(Note: This paragraph is optional.) Let's have our fathers stand up for a minute, so that we can see them. *(Turn to the congregation.)* Will the fathers of these children please stand up? *(Turn back to the children.)* Can you find your father? You may wave if you want to. *(Pause very briefly, then turn to the congregation.)* You may sit down; thank you. *(Turn back to the children.)*

Lesson

(Begin here if you do not use this lesson on Father's Day.)

Today we're going to talk about parents, both fathers and mothers. Let's start with fathers. How many of you have a father living at your house? *(Pause for response.)* Not all families have fathers, but many do.

What does your father do? *(Pause for response. Repeat the children's responses. Prompt them with questions to include all activities. Include both care-giving and disciplinary activities.)* Does your father make sure that you have food? Does your father make sure that you have clothes? Does your father make sure that you have a loving home? Does your father set some rules? Does he tell you what you may and may not do?

Some families don't have fathers at home. *(If children without fathers are present, direct your questions toward them. Pause for response after each question.)* Who makes sure that you have food? Who makes sure that you have clothes? Who sets the rules and tells you what you may or may not do?

All of you have some adult at home who takes care of you and who tells you what you may or may not do. Sometimes both fathers and mothers do that, sometimes only one adult. But they do take care of you, and they do set rules for you.

Why do your parents set rules for you? *(Pause for response.)* Because they love you, and they want you to grow up right. They don't want you to be hurt;

they want you to grow up strong and healthy. So they set rules and see that you follow the rules.

So, your parents love you, they care for you, and they set rules for you to follow. They expect you to obey them. That's what loving parents (*or* adults who love you) do.

There's someone else, someone who gave you parents (*or* adults) to love you, care for you, and set rules for you. There's someone who loves us all, cares for us all, and sets rules for all of us to follow. There's someone who is Father to everyone here. Who is that? *(Pause for response.)* Of course, God is our Father.

God says in the Bible, "You will be my sons and daughters." God is talking there to all Christians. God says that he loves us very much. God promises to take care of us. And God, as a loving Father, gives us rules to follow.

Can anyone think of some of the rules God wants us to follow? *(Pause for response. Prompt the children with questions.)* Does God tell us to help one another? Does God tell us to love one another? Does God say that the best rule is to love our neighbor as ourselves? Yes, those are some of the rules God wants us to follow.

Why does God set rules for us? *(Pause for response.)* Because he loves us and he wants us to live right. He doesn't want to see us hurt. He wants us to love him and love each other. So God, our Father, sets rules and expects us to obey them. That's what loving parents do.

God gave you parents (*or* adults who take care of you), didn't he? That's how God takes care of you. And often, that's how God lets you know the rules: through your parents.

Who gives the rules in your family? Does your father? Does your mother? Do they both? Does another adult? It doesn't really matter, does it? They give you rules because they love you. They're showing you how much God loves you.

Option

(Use this paragraph only on Father's Day.)

Since it's Father's Day today, make a special effort to honor your father. When you go home today, thank your father for taking care of you and for setting rules for you to follow.

Continue Lesson

Why not make a special effort today to say thank you to all adults who love you and take care of you? Make a special effort to follow the rules they set for you. And then say a little prayer of thanks to God your heavenly Father. Thank God for his love and care and for parents (*or* adults) who help you obey his rules.

21

Rejoice!

Scripture: Rejoice in the Lord always. I will say it again: Rejoice! (Phil. 4:4).

Concept: Be happy and praise God!

Object: A bouquet of flowers. Wildflowers would be best. (*Note:* It would be nice to have one flower for each child. If you do, use option 2.)

Look at these gorgeous flowers! *(Hold up the bouquet.)* Aren't they pretty? *(Pause for response.)* I picked them from a nearby field (*or* bought them) yesterday.

I think the flowers are especially pretty this time of year. When winter is past and spring comes, I'm happy. It's so nice to see flowers in bloom again.

That's why I picked these. They made me happy, and I thought that maybe they might make you happy, too. Seeing pretty bouquets of flowers like this often makes people happy.

While I picked these flowers, one verse from the Bible went through my head. Maybe it was because these flowers made me feel happy. Anyway, the verse I remembered says, "Rejoice in the Lord always. I will say it again: Rejoice!"

Can anyone tell me what it means to rejoice? *(Hold up the flowers.)* Maybe these happy flowers can give you a hint. *(Pause for response and repeat all responses.)* Yes, to rejoice means to be happy and to act happy. The Bible tells us to be happy in God.

As I picked these flowers *(hold up the bouquet),* they made me happy. I remembered that that's just what the Bible tells us to do, to be happy in God, who made these beautiful flowers.

We have all sorts of reasons to be happy in God. Can anyone tell me a reason to rejoice, or be happy in God? *(Pause for response. Repeat the children's responses. You may have to prompt them with the following questions.)* Does God love us? Yes, he does. That's a reason to rejoice in the Lord. Does God care for us? He's promised to care for us. That's another reason to rejoice. Who made these beautiful flowers? God did! Rejoice for the beautiful flowers. Who made this wonderful world? God did; rejoice in the Lord.

We can go on and on with reasons to rejoice, to be happy and praise God. There certainly are more reasons than there are flowers in this bouquet. *(As you state a few more reasons, pick out one flower at a time and hold it up.)* God gives us food. God gives us homes. God gives us sunlight. *(List some congregational reasons, e.g., God helped so-and-so back to health.)* God gave us Jesus to save us.

You get the idea, don't you? God gave us many, many reasons to rejoice—to be happy and praise him.

Option 1

(If you don't pass out flowers, finish with this paragraph.)

This week, when you go outside, look around and notice all the pretty flowers that are in bloom right now. Those pretty flowers can remind you to be happy and praise your God. Rejoice in the Lord always. Rejoice in the Lord this week!

Option 2

(If you pass out flowers, finish with this paragraph.)

I think there are enough flowers here so that each of you can take one home. I'd like you to put it in a glass of water so that you can enjoy it all week. Every time you look at it, remember to be happy and praise your God. You can rejoice in the Lord always. Rejoice in the Lord this week. *(Say,* "Rejoice in the Lord!" *to each child as you give him or her a flower.)*

22

Gifts

(Birthday)

Scripture: If you, then, though you are evil, know how to give good gifts to your children, how much more will your Father in heaven give good gifts to those who ask him! (Matt. 7:11).

Concept: God gives us good gifts.

Objects: A few empty boxes wrapped as gifts. (*Note:* This lesson can be used anytime as written. For a birthday, use option.)

Option

(If you plan to acknowledge a particular birthday, begin here.)

I know somebody who has a birthday this week. Can anyone guess who it is? *(Pause for response. Repeat responses.)* Probably several people will have birthdays soon, but I was thinking of (child's name). I know that his (*or* her) birthday is (the day). Happy birthday to (child's name)!

Lesson

(If you aren't acknowledging a particular birthday, begin here.)

Does anyone (else) have a birthday coming up this week? *(Pause for response. Acknowledge the children who respond.)* How about this month? Who has a birthday in June *(or whatever month it is)? (Pause for response and acknowledge the responses.)* And who has a birthday in July *(or the next month)? (Pause for response and acknowledge the responses.)* And who has a birthday coming up some time this year? *(Pause for response.)* Everybody does! We all have birthdays coming up some time or other, don't we? Yours may be this week or many weeks away, but you'll have a birthday some time.

What do you often get on your birthday? *(For option say,* What do you think [child's name] will get on his [her] birthday?) *(Pause for response. As you pause, put the gifts in front of you.)* Presents! Gifts!

How many of you like to open gifts? *(Pause for response. Unwrap and open one of the boxes as you speak.)* I think we all do. It's fun to wonder what's inside, take off the wrappings, then open the box to see your gift. *(Show the children the empty box.)* This is no gift at all, is it? *(Shake your head and pause for response.)*

You usually get much more than an empty box, don't you? *(Nod and pause for response.)* Of course! Do Mom and Dad sometimes give you some really good birthday presents? *(Nod and pause for response.)* What kinds of gifts do you get? *(Pause for response and repeat the responses.)* Those are really good gifts!

Most parents give their kids much more than empty boxes. *(Indicate the box.)* Parents know just what you need, so they can give you some really good gifts. *(Indicate the wrapped boxes.)*

Did you know that Jesus talked about gifts that your parents give you? *(Nod your head and pause for response.)* He did! Jesus said that just as parents know how to give good gifts to their kids, God knows how to give each one of us gifts that are better yet!

Does God give us gifts all wrapped up like this? *(Indicate a wrapped box and pause for response.)* No, of course not!

God doesn't wrap up anything he gives us, but God does give us things every single day. God doesn't even wait for our birthday. And Jesus says that the gifts God gives us are much better than birthday presents. *(Indicate the wrapped boxes.)*

Can you think of a gift that you get from God? What gifts does God give you every day? What do you get from God that's better than any birthday present? *(Pause for response and repeat the children's responses. You may have to prompt them with questions.)* Does God make sure you have enough food? enough clothes? Does God give you your parents, who give you such great gifts? Does God give you friends and relatives? Look outside: Does God give you nice sunny days? pretty flowers? a beautiful world? Does God give you things to make you happy? Does God give you love?

We could go on and on, couldn't we? God gives us all sorts of good things. God gives us everything we need. Every day God gives us good gifts.

Of course, they're not presents like these. *(Indicate the boxes.)* These are really extra gifts that people give us for our birthday. But the best gifts—everything we need to live and more, our families, friends, and even love—come to us from God.

So, these *(indicate the boxes)* can remind us of the really good gifts that we get from God. The next time you get a gift like this *(hold up a gift),* say thank you to the person who gave it to you. Then, while you unwrap it *(slowly unwrap the box as you speak),* think of all the good gifts that you get from God: friends, family, life, love. And, before you open your birthday gift *(do not open the box),* say thank you to God, who gives you every good gift.

Option

(If you have acknowledged a particular birthday, add the following paragraph.)

This week, say "Happy birthday" to (child's name). And when you do, remember that you *all* will receive good gifts from your loving God.

Fly Your Flag

(Patriotic Holiday)

Scripture: If you confess with your mouth, "Jesus is Lord," and believe in your heart that God raised him from the dead, you will be saved (Rom. 10:9).

Concept: We should *say* that Jesus is Lord.

Object: A flag of your nation. (*Note:* This lesson can be used anytime as written. For a patriotic holiday, use option.)

Option

(If you want to mention the holiday include the following paragraph.)

Who can tell me what holiday we're going to celebrate this week? *(Pause for response.)* Yes, the Fourth of July *(or whatever holiday)*. This week people will honor our country. We'll hear a lot of talk about what a great country this is, we'll see a lot of red, white, and blue *(or your country's colors),* we'll hear many good things said about (your country). People are proud to be citizens of (your country), and this week they'll let everyone know they are. Lots of people will proudly fly flags.

89

Lesson

(If you don't mention the holiday, begin here.)

Can anyone tell me what flag this is? *(Hold up the flag so that the children can see the whole thing.)* What country does this flag stand for? *(Pause for response.)* Yes, it's (<u>your country's</u>) flag. This flag stands for (<u>your country</u>).

People fly this flag to show that they're proud of our country. They love our country. They fly this flag to show that they're proud to be a citizen of (<u>your country</u>).

We all live in (<u>your country</u>), don't we? We're all citizens of (<u>your country</u>). But we belong to someone much bigger than just one country. We live in (<u>your country</u>), and we're loyal to it, but we belong, body and soul, to whom? *(Pause for response.)* Yes, to God (*or* Jesus). For now we live in (<u>your country</u>), but forever we belong to God's kingdom. We belong to Jesus, and Jesus is our Lord.

Are you proud that you belong to Jesus? Do you love Jesus? Do you want everyone to know that Jesus is your Lord? *(Nod your head and pause for response.)* Of course!

We're not ashamed of Jesus. Jesus is our Lord! We're proud to belong to Jesus. We can let the whole world know we do!

How can we let the world know that Jesus is our Lord? *(Pause for response. Repeat responses.)* There's one very simple way that we can let the world know that Jesus is Lord: Whenever we have a chance, we can tell someone that Jesus is our Lord.

90

In fact, the Bible says that we *should* tell people. God says that if we say with our mouth, "Jesus is Lord" and really believe it, we will be saved. Saying something with our mouth is called "confessing" it.

Jesus said that if we confess him before others, he will confess us before the Father. If we tell people that Jesus is our Lord and that we love him, Jesus will tell God the Father that he loves us.

Do you believe that Jesus is Lord? *(Nod your head and pause for response.)* Then tell others. Say, "Jesus is Lord."

Let's practice saying that a few times. Can you say it with me? Jesus is Lord! *(Speak slowly and indicate that the children should speak with you.)* Jesus is Lord! Jesus is Lord!

Saying that Jesus is Lord is like flying a flag. *(Hold up the flag.)* Someone flies this flag to let people know that they love this country. We say, "Jesus is Lord" to let people know that we love Jesus and belong to him.

I'd like you to do me a little favor this week. Look for flags. Every time you see a flag, fly your flag for Jesus. Say, "Jesus is Lord." Better yet, tell someone, "Jesus is Lord."

We may see lots of these flags *(hold up the flag)* flying this week. Then we can fly lots of flags for Jesus. Just say, "Jesus is Lord!"

24

Life's Lemons

(Tragic Event)

Scripture: And we know that in all things God works for the good of those who love him, who have been called according to his purpose (Rom 8:28).

Concept: God makes the bad events in our lives work for our good.

Objects: A lemon (cut in half), some sugar, a spoon, and a glass of water.

Who can tell me what this is? *(Hold up the lemon. Pause for response.)* Yes, it's a lemon. I brought it along today because I want to make some lemonade.

(Hold up the glass of water.) Here's the water; now I'll squeeze some lemon juice into it. *(Squeeze a few drops of juice into the water.)* That should give me some lemonade.

(Take a sip of the water and make a face.) That's not good at all. That's really sour. Imagine eating a lemon. *(Hold up the lemon.)* That's what this lemonade tastes like. It's terrible.

I think that I can fix it. *(Display the sugar.)* This will make it sweeter; then it might be good. *(Put some sugar into the lemonade, stir, and take another taste.)* That's much better.

Imagine that! I took something that tasted quite sour and made it taste good by adding sugar. *(Hold up the glass.)* The lemon juice is still in here, isn't it? I couldn't take that out. But I added sugar to make it taste better.

That's how we make lemonade. We take a sour mixture, change it a bit, and come up with something good.

The Bible tells us that God does the same thing in our lives. He doesn't make lemonade. But God does take the sad things that happen to us and make them good for us.

Sad things do happen sometimes. Maybe a friend moves away or a pet dies. Or maybe someone has a bad accident. *(If you have had a recent tragedy in the congregation, mention it here.)* We can't pretend those are good things *(or that's a good thing).* They're not *(or It isn't).* But they happen *(or it happened).*

(Hold up the glass of lemonade.) This glass of lemonade tasted terrible with just the lemon juice in it. But the juice was there; I couldn't get it out.

Just like the lemon juice in the water, sad things happen in our lives sometimes. We can't change those things. We can't undo something that has happened, just like I couldn't get the lemon juice out of the water.

Yet, God tells us that he will work the bad things out for our good. We may not know right away just how a bad thing will be good for us. But we know that God will make it work for our good.

(Take some more sugar and stir it into the lemonade.) God's work is like adding sugar to the lemon juice. We work it around a bit and the sour juice becomes much better. God works in our hearts, or in our lives, or some way to make bad things become good for us.

Sometimes, right after a sad thing happens, we can't possibly see how God can turn it to good. All we can say is, "That's a sad thing; it hurts." *(Refer directly to the event here and admit that it hurts.)*

But then we can think of this glass of lemon juice *(hold up the glass)* before I put in the sugar. It tasted terrible, and I didn't like it.

We can't change what happened, but we can add sugar. *(Hold up the sugar and put some more into the glass as you speak. Stir and keep stirring.)* And there is some way that God will turn the bad events in our lives into good. It may take a long, long time. We may not be able to see it happening. We may hurt for a long, long time. *(Keep stirring.)*

But we can remember that God is working. We don't always know how God works, but the Bible tells us he does, so we believe. God works all things in our lives—even bad things *(name the event)*—for our good. *(Take a sip of lemonade and smile.)*

25

Children of God

(Children's Day)

> **Scripture:** The Spirit himself testifies with our spirit that we are God's children (Rom. 8:16).
>
> **Concept:** Young and old Christians alike are children of God.
>
> **Objects:** The children, the congregation. (*Note:* This lesson can be used anytime as written. For Children's Day, use option.)

Option

(If you want to draw attention to Children's Day, include the following paragraph.)

Can anyone tell me what special day we're going to celebrate this week? *(Pause for response.)* Children's Day! That's just a made-up holiday. Some people celebrate Children's Day, some people don't. I just thought I'd mention it today because you may hear something about it this week.

Lesson

(If you don't mention Children's Day, begin here.)

Today we're going to talk about children and adults. Everybody begins life as a child and grows up to become an adult. We have both children and adults in church today.

Are you a child or an adult? *(Pause for response.)* Yes, you probably said that you're a child. People your age are usually called children.

How old must you be to be called an adult? Fifteen years old? Twenty-one years old? Fifty years old? Give me a guess. *(Pause for response and repeat responses.)*

To tell the truth, it's really difficult to know when someone becomes an adult. Some children act like adults when they're ten years old. Some adults act like children when they're fifty years old.

Some people say that you're an adult when you take care of yourself. When you have a job, buy your own food and clothes, supply your own needs— that's when some people say that you're an adult.

So look around once more. Do the people sitting here on the floor next to you have jobs or buy their own food or clothes? Are they adults? Do you take care of yourself? Are you an adult yet? *(Pause for response.)* No! I think we can safely say that you are children.

Now, look out at the congregation. Look toward where your parents are sitting. When you look out there, do you see adults? *(Pause for response.)* You do, don't you?

Well, I have a surprise for you. When I look out there, I see all children—all God's children.

Remember that I said you're an adult when you take care of yourself? Well, God's promised to take care of us forever. God takes care of adults as well as children.

Of course, when you grow up you learn to do some things for yourself. You get a job, you take care of your food and clothes, you even take care of children. But that doesn't mean that God will stop caring for you. God will call you his child and care for you forever.

Today, this week, this year, next year, and forever, you will always be a child of God. If you love Jesus, God will always care for you.

With God, every Christian—young or old alike—is a child. *(Gesture to the congregation and the children.)* Everybody here—young and old—is God's child. No matter how old you become, you will always be God's child.

Option

(Include this paragraph only if you have mentioned Children's Day.)

So, go ahead and celebrate Children's Day this week. But when you do, celebrate with everyone in your home, because we all—young and old alike—are God's children.

26

The Camera's Running!

Scripture: Nothing in all creation is hidden from God's sight. Everything is uncovered and laid bare before the eyes of him to whom we must give account (Heb. 4:13).

Concept: God sees everything that we do.

Object: A video camera.

I've got my video camera here today. *(Hold up the video camera.)* Shall I take some film of you? *(Pretend to.)* Are you ready? Smile! Act nice for the video! *(Film the children or pretend to film them. Put the camera down before you proceed.)*

That should make (*or* would have made) a good video. Everyone smiled so nicely. Everyone was so good.

There's a strange thing about people and cameras that I want you to notice. As soon as someone brings out a camera, everyone who's going to have his or her picture taken smiles. *(Smile almost too brightly.)* They may be crabby before *(frown)*, but they'll smile for the camera. *(Smile brightly again.)*

The same thing happens with video cameras. Even naughty kids behave really well when the video camera comes out. *(Display the camera.)* You're not naughty kids; you're good. But even you are *especially* good for the camera, aren't you? *(Nod and pause for response.)*

Sometimes we may make faces or act a little silly for a video. That's because we're a little bit nervous when the camera's running. But do you ever do anything really bad in front of a camera? Do you ever hit anyone, or bite, or maybe steal something in front of a video camera? *(Shake your head and pause for response.)* Of course not!

We want people to see us at our best. We don't want people to see us do something bad. So when the camera's running, we'll act our best.

Did you know that there's always a video camera running, and it's always pointed right at us? *(Pause for effect. Pick up the camera and point it at children as you speak.)* It's pointed at you, and you, and you, and you.

That sounds silly, doesn't it? There isn't really a big camera in the sky pointed at us. But there is someone watching us all of the time, seeing and remembering everything that we do.

Who is watching us all of the time? *(Pause for response.)* Yes, God is. God can see everything. The Bible says that nothing in all of creation is hidden from God. He sees everything that we do, all of the time.

So it is sort of like a video camera that's running all the time. God sees everything and remembers everything. It's as if everything we do is on video.

Does that mean that we should be good all of the time? *(Nod and pause for response.)* Of course. But God doesn't want you to be good just because he's watching. God wants you to be good because you love him. But he does see everything that you do. It's like the camera's always running.

I don't mean that to sound scary to you, because that should be very comforting. God not only watches you, God watches *over* you. You are never out of his sight, because he loves you so.

I'd guess that your parents are rather like God in that way, aren't they? They watch you and watch over you because they love you.

I'd guess that they like to take pictures of you, too. How many of your parents have cameras at home? *(Raise your hand as an example and pause for response.)* I'd guess that some of those are even video cameras, aren't they?

So, the next time your parents or someone else takes a picture or a video of you, listen carefully. They may say, "Smile, the camera's on." And that can remind you of God's "video." His "camera" is always on, because he's always watching you and always watching over you.

27

No Bad Videos

Scripture: For I will forgive their wickedness and will remember their sins no more (Heb. 8:12).

Concept: God edits our actions through Christ.

Objects: The video camera from last week, at least four bits of old videotape, a wastebasket. (*Note:* This lesson should be done the week after "The Camera's Running.")

Can anyone tell me what these are? *(Show the children the bits of videotape.)* Maybe you don't know; not many people see these.

(Show the children the camera while you speak.) Maybe this will help you. We had this here last week. What's this? *(Pause for response.)* That's right, this is a video camera. Last week we talked about how God sees everything we do, as if he's taking a video.

(Hold up the camera and the bits of tape. Indicate each as you speak.) If this is the video camera, what do you think this is? *(Pause for response.)* That's right, this is videotape. This is some videotape that I used in this camera.

But I didn't like part of what I filmed. I made some mistakes on the tape. Do you know what I did? I cut out this part of the tape. I kept only the good parts.

I'm going to throw these bad parts away. *(Throw some of the videotape into the wastebasket.)*

There! Now I've thrown the bad parts away, and I'll forget about them. I have only good videos left at home.

Throwing the bad parts away is called *editing.* I've edited my videotape by cutting out the bad parts and leaving only the good parts. Because I've edited my tape I have only good videotape left.

Editing is a fun thing to do: throwing out the bad and keeping only the good. If I make a mistake I can edit it, or cut it, out of my tape. *(Throw some more videotape into the wastebasket as you speak.)*

(Hold up the video camera again.) What did we say about this video camera last week? Who sees everything we do? *(Pause for response.)* That's right, God does!

But, do you know what? God edits, too! *(Hold up some videotape.)* God sees the bad pictures, the bad things we do; but he cuts them right out of the tape and throws all those bad things away. *(Throw the tape into the wastebasket.)*

God tells us in the Bible that he will not remember our sins. If we love Jesus, God will take all our sins, our bad videos, and throw them away. *(Throw some more tape away.)* Then God will have only our good videos; God will remember only the good we do.

That doesn't mean that we can go out and do bad things all the time, does it? If we love Jesus, we'll try to be good. But we all make mistakes sometimes. God promises us that he'll forget our mistakes. He won't remember our sins. If we love Jesus, all our sins are forgotten.

So, the next time you see a videotape, watch it closely. Are there any parts in it you don't like? Ask an adult if someone could edit them and cut them out. Then tell that adult that God edits our sins and cuts them all out of our life if we love Jesus.

If you see a video that you think is perfect, with no bad parts, remember that God cuts the sins out of your life and throws them away *(throw the last bit of videotape away)* to make you perfect. If you love Jesus, you're perfect in God's sight.

28

More Special than Sparrows

Scripture: Are not five sparrows sold for two pennies? Yet not one of them is forgotten by God. Indeed, the very hairs of your head are all numbered. Don't be afraid; you are worth more than many sparrows (Luke 12:6–7).

Concept: God watches over each of his children.

Object: A picture of a sparrow. (*Note:* The picture must be of a sparrow. A colored picture will work better than black and white. Check any bird book for one.)

Do any of you know names of different birds? Those bright red birds we see are cardinals. Those bold blue ones are blue jays. What kind is this bird? *(Hold up the picture for all to see.)* Who can tell me the name of this common bird? *(Pause for response.)* Yes, it's a sparrow.

Almost everyone knows sparrows. Sparrows live in all parts of the world; they're very common birds. Sometimes lots of sparrows live in one area and people think that they're pesky birds. We have sparrows around here. How many of you have seen sparrows? *(Pause for response.)* Good!

This week, I want you all to look for sparrows. I'll show you this picture again so that you're sure what they look like. *(Take the picture and walk around with it so that all the children can see it. Continue to speak as you walk.)* Look closely at the picture. A sparrow is a medium-sized bird, not as big as a cardinal or a blue jay. Its a rather plain bird; its feathers are mostly brown. Sparrows live around here. This week, I'd like you to notice birds and look especially for sparrows.

I want you to especially notice sparrows because Jesus talked about sparrows. They were common birds where Jesus lived, too. Everybody knew what Jesus was talking about whenever he mentioned sparrows.

Jesus said that God watches over his sparrows so closely that he knows when one of the birds falls! There are so many sparrows in the world; yet God knows when only one of the little birds falls. That's how closely God watches over his creatures.

And that's why I want you to look for sparrows this week. When you see one you can tell yourself that God is watching over that same little bird that you're looking at. That's what Jesus said.

But Jesus didn't stop there. He said that we, God's children, are much more valuable to God than his sparrows.

So, if God watches over every sparrow, and we are more valuable to God than sparrows, does God watch over us? *(Nod and pause for response.)* Of course he does. God watches over each one of us. God watches over you and you and you and you. *(Point to individual children as you speak.)* Jesus said so.

You are God's child, his special creature. He knows everything about you, he loves you very much, and he's always watching over you. That's what Jesus said.

I would like you to look at this picture of a sparrow very closely again. *(Walk the picture around again. Continue to speak as you do so.)* This is the bird to look for this week. It's a common, little, brown bird—a sparrow. You'll probably see lots of sparrows if you look for them. Every time you see a sparrow you can remember that God is watching over that bird, and God is surely watching over you!

29

Oops!

Scripture: He who guards his mouth and his tongue keeps himself from calamity (Prov. 21:23).

Concept: Words once spoken cannot be recalled.

Objects: A tube of toothpaste, a toothbrush, a small cloth.

Who can tell me what this is? *(Spread the small cloth over your demonstration area, then hold up the tube of toothpaste. Pause for response.)* It's toothpaste! We all use toothpaste when we brush our teeth.

You know how to use toothpaste, don't you? *(Pause slightly.)* Of course! *(Hold up the toothbrush, then position the tube of toothpaste over it.)* You squeeze a little onto your toothbrush before you brush your teeth. *(Mimic squeezing the tube and brushing your teeth.)*

Let's do it again. *(Squeeze a little too much.)* Oops! Too much toothpaste! We've all done that, haven't we?

This mess reminds me of an imaginary game some people play with their toothpaste. Maybe you'd like to try it.

How many of you brush your teeth before you go to bed at night? *(Pause for response.)* Good, then you can use your imagination when you brush your teeth tonight.

(Hold up the tube of toothpaste.) Pretend that you are this tube of toothpaste. *(Point to the cap.)* Here's your head. *(Point to the bottom.)* These are your feet— rather strange feet, but we're just pretending. *(Point to the length of the tube.)* This is you, the pretend you.

Inside are all the things that you think. There are thoughts and words and feelings jumbled up and stuffed inside of you, just like the toothpaste in this tube.

Sometimes all those words and thoughts and feelings come out as words *(take the cap off and point to the hole)* from your mouth. *(Squeeze a little toothpaste out.)* Here they come, words out of your mouth.

That's fine, but you should be careful. Sometimes you say a little too much. *(Squeeze a little too much toothpaste out with each sentence.)* Maybe you're angry at someone and call him or her a name. Oops! Maybe you gossip about someone. Oops! Maybe you tell a little lie. Oops! You said some angry or hurtful words. They just came out of your mouth. Oops!

Let's try to fix it. *(Try to scrape up a little toothpaste with the tube.)* This doesn't work, does it? You can't put the toothpaste back into the tube. When it's out, it's out forever.

Squeezing out too much toothpaste is just like saying angry, hurtful, gossipy words. Once you've said them, you can't take them back. You can try. *(Mimic trying to put toothpaste back into the tube.)* You can say, "I'm sorry." You can apologize for angry words. But you can never take those words back. Someone has heard them. Someone has been hurt by them, and you can't change that.

The Bible tells us that we should be careful with our words. God tells us that words can do a lot of damage. He tells us that wise people think before they speak but fools gush out words. God tells us that watching what we say can keep us out of a lot of trouble.

(Hold up the tube of toothpaste.) Watching what we say is like not squeezing too hard. *(Squeeze more toothpaste from the tube.)* Toothpaste out of the tube can't be put back. Words out of your mouth can't be taken back. The damage is done. Think before you speak.

Now you have a handy little reminder. *(Hold up the tube of toothpaste.)* When you brush your teeth tonight, think about what you're doing. Don't squeeze out too much toothpaste; you can't put it back.

Be very careful when you speak, so that you never have to say, "Oops!" *(Squeeze out a little more toothpaste, then cover your open mouth.)*

30

Me Last!

Scripture: If anyone wants to be first, he must be
the very last, and the servant of all (Mark 9:35).

Concept: Let others go first.

Object: The children. (*Note:* As the children
come forward, tell them to remain standing
and to form a line. Help the children form a
straight line, one behind another, all facing
you. The first in line should be nearest you;
the last should be farthest away.)

Who's at the front of this line? Who's
first? *(Pause for response.)* Yes, you people *(indicate a
few children in the front of the line)* are first. (<u>Name of
the child at the head of the line</u>) is the very first one.

You people *(indicate the children at the rear of the
line)* are in the back. Sorry about that. You're last.

But you *(brightly indicate the children at the head of
the line)* are in front. You're first.

Let's sit down now and talk about that arrangement
a little bit. *(Take your accustomed seats.)*

When you get into a line like that, where's the
best place to be, first or last? Where in line do people
like to be? *(Pause for response.)* Most people like to be
first, don't they? It's natural to want to be first.

It's so natural that we often hear this: "Me first! Me first! Me first!" *(Use an excited voice, as a child would.)* I'm glad I didn't hear any of that today; sometimes we do.

When someone passes out treats to a crowd, what do some people say? *(Pause and indicate that they should answer.)* "Me first!" That's right.

When you play games with other kids and you have to take turns, what do some people say? *(Pause for response.)* "Me first!" That's it! Everyone wants to be first.

Have you ever said, "Me first!"? *(Nod and pause for response.)* Yes, I think we all do sometimes. If we don't say it, we think it: *Me first!*

Let's say it one more time: Me first! *(Pause for response.)* There, we said it; I hope that's the last time we'll ever say "Me first!"

Jesus would rather have us say "Me last!" Jesus told us not to put ourselves first. We should put others before ourselves. We should let them take the best spots; we should let them have the places of honor. In other words, we should say "Me last!"

That sounds strange to us, doesn't it? We're not used to hearing "Me last!"

Let's try saying it a few times. *(Indicate that you want the children to speak with you.)* Me last! Me last! Me last!

So, when you line up to go someplace, should you push to the front or let others go first? *(Pause for response.)* Let others go first. Me last!

When someone passes out treats, should you try to get the first piece? *(Pause for response.)* No, let others fight for that. Me last!

When you play games, should you take the first turn? *(Pause for response.)* No; let others go first. Me last!

What's a good little rule to follow? *(Pause for response.)* That's right: Me last!

In fact, Jesus said that people who put themselves last are really first in his sight. He said that the first shall be last and the last shall be first. So where's the best place to be if you want to please Jesus? *(Pause for response.)* That's right: last!

Now we're going to line up to go back to our seats. Who wants to be first? *(Pause for response.)* And who wants to be last? *(Pause for response.)*

Me last! I'll line you up this time so that no one argues about being first or last. *(Line the children up in a straight line as before but face the congregation so that no one is first or last.)* There, a straight line with no one first or last.

But just so that you'll remember, let's do this one more time. *(Go to one side of the line and face the children.)* Can you stay in line but turn to face me?

Now we have a first and a last, just as we did before. *(Speak to the first children in line.)* I know you didn't choose this place. Who's first in this line? *(Indicate that the first children should raise their hands.)* And who's last? Who's way near the end? *(Walk to the other side of the line while you speak.)* But in Jesus' eyes, everyone who is last shall be first. Turn around and face me. See that? The last are first.

If you want to be first for Jesus, what do you say? *(Pause for response.)* That's right: "Me last!"

31

What a Deal!

Scripture: For it is by grace you have been saved, through faith—and this not from yourselves, it is the gift of God—not by works, so that no one can boast (Eph. 2:8–9).

Concept: Salvation is free.

Objects: Pictures of various items for sale with prices included on the pictures. Newspaper advertisements are fine. Be sure to pick items of interest to children—snacks, toys, clothes, bikes, etc.

I'm going shopping tomorrow, so I cut a few ads out of the newspaper. I want to get some good deals, but I've noticed that almost everything is expensive lately. You must pay for what you get.

Let me read you some of these prices. Here are a few candy bars. They're on sale for (the price). I'd like some of those. Here's a game I've always wanted. I can get it for (the price). I'm willing to pay that price; I really want that game. *(Continue in this manner until you have identified approximately 2/3 of the items. Start with the least expensive item and work your way up.)*

Do you see what I mean when I say that you pay for what you get? The bigger, better things I want are more expensive. Sometimes I just can't afford them.

You probably have heard your parents say that, haven't you? *(Nod and pause for response.)* Maybe you've asked them for a new bike or an expensive toy and they've said, "No, we can't afford that." They probably really want to get it for you, but it costs too much.

Look at this bike *(or one of the more expensive items),* for example. I would like it, but it costs too much. *(Name the price.)* I won't get it. Or this car. This costs (the price). That's a lot of money. If I wanted to move into this new house I might have to pay (a price). That's way too much. I can't pay that price. *(Identify the remaining items in this manner. Comment about how nice or good each is but that it's just too expensive. The price is too high.)*

That's just the way it is; the bigger and better something is, the more it costs. Sometimes the price is really very high. But then, you pay for what you get—usually.

There is one thing that we can get absolutely free, and it just happens to be the most valuable thing in the world. In fact, it's worth more than everything else in the world.

What is it? Salvation. God tells us in the Bible that we can have salvation free.

Salvation is a big word. Just think of heaven. If you have salvation, you are going to heaven some day. Everything will be perfect, forever. If you have salvation, you have heaven. And God says in the Bible that you can have heaven free.

Remember that I said you must pay for what you get? *(Pause briefly.)* Who do you think paid for heaven? *(Pause for response.)* That's right, Jesus did. Jesus paid the price of heaven so that we can have it free. And heaven is so big and so good it cost more than anything. It cost Jesus his life. Jesus paid that cost for our salvation. It's a free gift from him.

Maybe here in (<u>name of your city or area</u>) we have to pay for what we get. That's what the newspaper tells us *(hold up the clippings)* every day. When we get things, we're always reminded that we must pay for them.

That's OK because now, every time that we go shopping or even ask about a price or see a price tag, we can think about the free gift God gives us. If our parents ever say that they can't afford something we want, that's OK too, because the best gift you can ever, ever have is heaven. And heaven is free, from God, through Jesus, for us.

32

Patchwork People

(Ethnic Diversity)

Scripture: I now realize how true it is that God does not show favoritism but accepts men from every nation who fear him and do what is right (Acts 10:34–35).

Concept: Ethnic background means nothing to God. We are all one in Christ.

Objects: A box of crayons containing at least red, yellow, black, white, and brown; an uncolored picture of a person (this can be crudely drawn, as long as it is recognizable as a person). Optional: a copy of the picture for each child. (*Note:* This lesson can be used as written anytime or at a celebration of ethnic diversity.)

I'm going to color a picture while we're talking. *(Put the picture on the floor in front of you. Show the children the crayons.)* I'll show it to you when I'm finished. But first, I want to know if you like certain colors.

(Take out the red crayon.) How many of you like red? *(Pause for response, then use the red crayon to color one part of the picture as you speak.)* I like red, too. It's such a bright color. I'll color part of the picture red.

(Take out the black crayon.) How many of you like black? Is black your favorite color? *(Pause for response, then use the black crayon to color one part of the picture as you speak.)* Not as many people like black, do they? But it's an important color.

(Continue in the same manner with yellow, white, and brown. Comment on the color as you use it. Be sure to mention favorite and not-so-favorite colors. When you are finished with the five colors, you should have a "patchwork person," e.g., a brown leg, a yellow leg, a red arm, a black arm, etc.)

There, I'm finished with the picture; it's a beauty! Would you like to see it? *(Show it to the children.)*

I'll call this my patchwork person. It looks like God patched it all together. It looks like God took a brown leg and a yellow leg, a red arm and a black arm, and put them on a brown body.

Does God ever do that? Does God make people with different colors of skin on different parts of their bodies? *(Pause for response.)* No; at least I haven't seen any.

But God does make people of different colors, doesn't he? Most of us are (<u>whatever color</u>). African Americans are called blacks. Some people think that Chinese are yellow. Other Asians are sort of brown. Native Americans are sometimes called red people. People from Europe are called whites.

(Hold up the picture again.) That's why I colored this person red, yellow, black, white, and brown. My patchwork person has all colors of skin to stand for all colors of people.

117

(Keep the picture up.) As I colored this, we mentioned favorite colors and not-so-favorite colors. I think more of you liked red than black. White *(or another)* wasn't such a favorite either.

Do you think that God has favorite skin colors? *(Pause for response.)* I don't think so either. Red, yellow, black, white, and brown are all the same to God.

The Bible tells us that God doesn't have favorites. God accepts people from every nation. As long as someone believes in Jesus, he or she is God's child. God loves all his children.

(Hold up the picture again.) So this patchwork person can remind you of all of God's children. Some are red, some black, some white, some yellow, and some are brown. God loves them all; color doesn't make any difference to him.

Do you think the color of a person's hair makes a difference to God? *(Pause for response.)* Of course not! How about the color of a person's eyes? Does God have a favorite eye color? *(Pause for response.)* No! Does it matter to God if your eyes are round or slanted? *(Pause for response.)* No! Does it matter to God if your lips are thick or thin? *(Pause for response.)* Of course not!

The only thing that matters to God is if you love Jesus. Anyone of any color who loves Jesus is God's child.

(Hold up the picture again.) If this patchwork person were real and loved Jesus, would all these colors together make a difference? *(Pause for response.)* Of course not. God has no favorite color of people.

You'll probably never see a patchwork person like this. *(Indicate the picture.)* But you will see people who are different colors from yourself. And then you can remind yourself that color doesn't make any difference to God, so it shouldn't to us. Red, yellow, black, white, brown; if we love Jesus, we are all God's children.

Option

(Add the following paragraph if you have brought pictures for each of the children.)

I've brought pictures for you to take home and color. *(Hold up an uncolored picture.)* Use any color that you want to use, or make a patchwork person if you want to. When you pick a favorite color, you can remember that God doesn't have any favorite colors of people. When you're finished, hang it up where you can see it. It can remind you that people of every color belong to God.

33

Soap for Our Sins

Scripture: Whoever believes in the Son has eternal life, but whoever rejects the Son will not see life, for God's wrath remains on him (John 3:36).

Concept: Only Jesus can remove our sins.

Object: A bar of soap, stains on your hands.

My hands became dirty on the way to church. *(Show the children the stains on your hands.)* I should wash them to remove the stains.

Maybe I can just blow the dirt away. *(Blow on the dirty spots.)* Do you think that will help? *(Pause for response.)* I don't think so either. You can't blow these dirty hands clean. *(Display your hands again.)* Still dirty!

Maybe I can clean them by rubbing them on my clothes. *(Rub your hands lightly on your clothes as you speak.)* Do you think that will help? *(Pause for response.)* I don't think so either; my hands are quite dirty. *(Display your hands again.)* The stains are still there.

Maybe I should run a little water over them. Do you think that water alone will help? *(Pause for response.)* I don't think so; these stains are really ground into my hands.

I need one special thing to help wash these stains away; who can tell me what it is? I must wet them with water so that this one thing works, but I can't get these stains off without what and water? *(Pause for response.)*

Of course, I need soap. *(Hold up the bar of soap.)* If I want to clean all the stains off my hands, I need to use soap. Only soap will do. If I don't use soap, the stains will remain on my hands.

How many of you have ever gotten your hands dirty? *(Pause for response.)* Everyone, of course. Everyone gets their hands dirty once in a while.

How many of you have used soap to clean your hands? *(Pause for response.)* Everyone! Sure, everyone uses soap to clean their dirty hands. *(Hold up the bar of soap and pretend to wash your hands as you speak.)* Use soap when you wash your hands, and all the stains disappear.

But there are some stains, some dirt, that soap won't remove. They're like the stains on our hands, but soap won't make them go away.

God tells us that we are stained by sin. That's picture language. It means that we all have some sin in us that God doesn't like to see. *(Hold up your hands.)* We don't like to see stains on our hands; God doesn't like to see stains of sin on us.

Nobody's perfect. Nobody does only good things and says only good things all the time. We all do bad things once in a while, and we all say bad things once in a while. We may be sorry later, but we did it. We said or did a bad thing. That's a sin.

Our sins are like the stains on our hands. *(Display your hands again.)* They're dirty spots on us, spots that *must* come out.

There's only one thing that takes these spots off my hands; what is that? *(Pause for response.)* Yes, the soap. *(Hold up the soap.)*

And there's only one person who can take away the stains of our sins. Who's that? Who died on a cross to save us from our sins? *(Pause for response.)* Yes, Jesus! The Bible tells us that only Jesus can remove the stains of our sins. Only Jesus will do. If we believe in Jesus, God sees no stains on us.

Can you stop sinning all by yourself? *(Pause for response.)* No! Can your parents take away your sins? *(Pause for response.)* Can the minister take away your sins? *(Pause for response.)* NO! Only Jesus can take away your sins. Love Jesus, and God sees you as perfectly clean.

Now, we can't say that Jesus is a bar of soap. *(Hold up the soap.)* He's much, much more than that. But we can say that a bar of soap reminds us of Jesus. Only soap can take the stains off my hands. *(Display your hands.)* Only Jesus can take the stain of sin from my life.

So, the next time you use soap to wash yourself, who are you going to think about? *(Pause for response.)* Jesus! Only Jesus can remove your sins. Love Jesus, and you become completely clean!

34

Speak Up!

(Mission Emphasis)

Scripture: How, then, can they call on the one they have not believed in? And how can they believe in the one of whom they have not heard? And how can they hear without someone preaching to them? (Rom. 10:14).

Concept: We must tell others about Jesus.

Object: A speaker, disconnected from a sound system (a "boom box" with disconnected speakers would be great. Take the boom box also); a Bible. (*Note:* This lesson can be used anytime as written. The option for specific mission emphasis use is included at the end of the lesson.)

I have a strange box with me today. Each of you probably has used one of these, although you didn't know you were using it. You probably have a box somewhat like this at home. *(Hold up the speaker. Place it where everyone can see it.)*

I'll give you a minute to guess what it is. Does anyone think he or she knows? *(Pause for response. Repeat responses.)* Time's up. I didn't think you'd guess, because we usually don't notice these things. This is called a speaker.

All radios, TVs, and tape decks *(or whatever)* have speakers. Some speakers aren't this large. Radios and TVs often have speakers right inside them. Sometimes the speakers are attached to the side, and you can take them off. This speaker came from my boom box *(or whatever system)*.

Option 1

(If there are speakers visible in the sanctuary, add this paragraph.)

We even have speakers here, but we hardly ever notice them. *(Point to the speakers.)* Those speakers are for the sound system in this room.

Continue Lesson

This speaker *(indicate the speaker)* is very important. The sound from my boom box *(or whatever system)* comes through here. Without the speaker, I can't hear my boom box *(or whatever system)*.

This speaker doesn't *make* the music. My radio *(or whatever system)* does that. This makes the music loud enough to hear. I can't hear what's in my boom box *(or whatever system)* without the speaker.

We can't hear what's on TV without the speaker inside the set. We can't hear what's on a radio without the speaker. The music may be there, but we can't hear it. We need the speaker.

124

Option 2

(If you are using a boom box, use this paragraph.)

Let me show you. *(Make sure both speakers are disconnected and volume is low. Then turn on the boom box.)* You can't hear it, can you? We need a speaker. *(Connect one speaker and turn it on again.)* Now you can hear it. The music *(or whatever)* is coming through the speaker.

Option 3

(If you have pointed out the speakers in the sanctuary and have made the following arrangements, use this paragraph.)

Let me show you. *(Signal the sound person to turn off the sound. Say a few words to the children.)* Do you think the people in the back of the room can hear that? No! They need the speaker. *(Signal the sound person to turn on the sound.)* Now, do you think they can hear this? Of course; we have the speaker connected.

Continue Lesson

A speaker is very important, isn't it? It carries the sound. We can't hear what's going on in the boom box *(or whatever system)* without it. How can we hear without a speaker? *(Ask the question slowly, pointedly; but don't pause for response.)* We can't.

God asks us the same question in the Bible. God asks how people can hear without a speaker.

Do you think God means a speaker like this? *(Indicate your speaker and pause for response.)* Of course not! God means a real, live person, a person who speaks.

God asks us how people can hear his Word if nobody speaks it. *(Hold up the Bible.)* Here's God's Word. Does it talk? *(Pause for response.)* Of course not. You must read it, or someone must read it to you.

And if people don't have a Bible and don't know about Jesus *(put the Bible behind you),* how can they find out about him? *(Pause for response.)* That's right. Someone must tell them. Someone must be a speaker and speak up about Jesus.

This boom box *(or whatever system)* doesn't do much good if people can't hear it. It needs a speaker. The story of Jesus does no good if people can't hear about him. How can they hear without a speaker? Someone must speak up and tell the story of Jesus.

Who, do you think, can be speakers? Who can talk about Jesus? *(Raise your hand and pause for response.)* Of course, we all can. We all speak in different ways, but we all can, at some time, tell people about Jesus.

How can people hear without a speaker? They can't. Who can speak? *(Pause for response.)* We can! We can tell others *(hold up the Bible)* the Bible stories of Jesus.

Option

(If you are using this lesson for a mission emphasis service, add the following paragraph.)

What about people whom we don't know? Suppose there are people downtown *(or in another town, or state, or country—whatever your emphasis is)* who don't know about Jesus and have no one to tell them? How can we speak to them? *(Pause for response. Repeat responses.)*

We can send Bibles, and we can send speakers! That's right, we can help send our missionaries. Our missionaries are God's speakers *(indicate the speaker)* to tell the story of Jesus.

Continue Lesson

Right here at home, with our friends, we can be God's speakers *(indicate the speaker)* to tell others what's in the Bible. *(Indicate the Bible.)*

I'd like you to do something with speakers sometime this week. Look around your house and your car for speakers *(indicate the speaker)*—this kind. Ask an adult to help you find them. See if you can count the number of speakers you have both in your house and in your car.

Then, every time you find a speaker, try to think of one way you can be a speaker for God. (Option: Try to think of one missionary whose name you know.) You'll probably find a lot of speakers *(indicate the speaker)*—this kind. I hope we also have a lot of speakers for Jesus. How can people hear without a speaker?

35

Who Are You?

(Reformation Day)

Scripture: You perceive my thoughts from afar (Ps. 139:2).

Concept: God knows who we really are.

Object: A face mask that looks like a character the children can identify. (*Note:* Although this lesson mentions neither Reformation Day nor Halloween, it works best when used near the end of October.)

What's this? *(Hold up the mask. Pause for response.)* That's right, it's a face mask. You've probably seen many of these lately.

(Put the mask on your face.) Who am I supposed to look like? *(Pause for response. Repeat all responses.)* That's right, Mickey Mouse *(or whomever)*.

Can you tell who I am with this mask on? Can you tell what I'm really like behind this mask? *(Shake your head and pause for response.)* Of course not! I'm covering my face with a mask. I have to take it off *(take off the mask)* before you can see the real me.

This week (*or* On Halloween) some kids (*or* you) will put on whole costumes with masks or face paint and try to look like someone else. We'll see all sorts of characters walking the streets.

Can we tell who those kids really are? *(Put the mask on briefly.)* Do you always know who's behind the mask? *(Shake your head and pause for response.)* No! Sometimes we have to ask them, "Who are you?"

Sometimes it's fun to put on a mask and fool people. You know that you've really fooled them when they say, "Who are you?"

Sometimes we fool people without putting a mask on. We put on a pretend mask. We pretend to be something that we really aren't at all.

Let me explain. Sometimes, I feel really sad about something. *(Look sad.)* But I don't want people to know, so I smile and act happy. *(Smile brightly.)* Sometimes I may be scared or nervous. *(Look frightened.)* But I don't want people to know, so I act really brave. *(Look confident.)* That's a "mask" I put on. I want people to think I'm happy and brave, so I act that way. *(Put the mask on briefly.)* People don't see the real me. People don't know that I'm sad and scared.

Do you ever act one way when you feel different inside? Do you ever act big and bold when you really feel little and scared? *(Nod your head and pause for response.)* I think we all do sometimes. Then people don't know the real us. We've put on a mask. *(Put the mask up to your face briefly.)*

Do people always ask, "Who are you?" or "How do you really feel inside?" *(Shake your head and pause for response.)* No! They think they know us because of the way we act. They don't know that we're putting on a mask *(hold the mask up to your face briefly),* that we're putting on a show.

But one person knows. God can see right through our masks to the real person inside. God knows when we're putting on a show. God tells us that he looks at our hearts and knows exactly how we feel. We can act big and bold and fool people; but if we feel small and frightened, God knows.

I think that's great! God knows you and exactly how you feel inside. God loves you, cares about you, and wants to help you. He wants to help you just the way you are, so he looks at your heart. You can't fool God with a mask. *(Put the mask in front of your face and keep it there.)*

This week, when you see people with masks on, you may have to ask them, "Who are you?" You may even put on a mask to fool people. They won't know the real you.

All these masks can remind you that you can't fool God. God looks right through any mask *(take off the mask)* at your heart. God knows exactly how you feel inside. God knows and loves the real you.

36

Who's Your Leader?

(Election Day)

Scripture: You did not choose me, but I chose you and appointed you to go and bear fruit—fruit that will last (John 15:16).

But we ought always to thank God for you, brothers loved by the Lord, because from the beginning God chose you to be saved through the sanctifying work of the Spirit and through belief in the truth (2 Thess. 2:13).

Concept: God chose us.

Object: A ballot. If you cannot obtain an official ballot, you can make one. Use names of well-known leaders. You will have to adjust what you say to the type of ballot you have. (*Note:* This lesson can be used anytime as written. For Election Day, use option.)

Option

(If you wish to mention an upcoming election, begin here.)

Can anyone tell me about a special thing that will happen this week? *(Pause for response. Repeat responses.)* We're going to have an election! Next Tuesday is Election Day. Adults will vote for certain people to be our leaders.

Lesson

(If you don't mention an upcoming election, begin here.)

I've brought a ballot with me today. Children don't often see ballots. This is what we use to elect our leaders. *(Hold up the ballot so that all the children can see it.)*

Here are the names of the people who want to be our president *(or prime minister or whatever. Read the names as you point to them).* Whoever wants (a candidate's name) to be president *(or whatever)* puts a little check in front of that name. Whoever wants (another candidate's name) to be president *(or whatever)* puts a check in front of that name.

All the checks are counted. Whoever gets the most checks will be president *(or whatever)*. Most of the people voted for that person. Whoever gets the most votes wins. That's how we choose our leaders.

That's how we chose (name of your current president or prime minister). More people voted for (name) than for anyone else, so (name) has been our leader.

We respect (name of the leader), and we obey our laws; but we Christians have a much more important leader, don't we? We have someone who will always be our leader. Who is that? Who is our heavenly leader? *(Pause for response.)* Of course, God will always be our leader.

Did we vote for God? Did we choose him as our leader? *(Shake your head and pause for response.)* No! We didn't choose God, God chose us!

The Bible says that God chose us from the beginning of time. Jesus said to his disciples, "You did not choose me, but I chose you." God chose us to be his followers.

That's like (name of your president or prime minister) calling you on the telephone and saying, "(Name of a child), I want to be your leader."

Did (name of that leader) ever call you? *(Pause for response.)* Probably not.

Does (name of that leader) even know you? *(Pause for response.)* I doubt it. (Name) is a very important, busy person. Important people like that don't often call people like us. We choose them to be our leaders. They don't choose us to be their followers.

But God chose us! God, who knows everything and can do anything, chose us to follow him. God's the most important person there ever was and ever will be, and he chose to love us and lead us. God is our loving leader because he wants to be and he chose to be!

Right now you're too young to mark a ballot like this. *(Hold up the ballot.* Option: You're too young to vote in the election this week.) You're too young to choose a leader.

But you're never too young to be chosen by God. God already chose you as his own. How fortunate you are to have a loving God choose you to be his follower!

Who is our president (*or* prime minister)? *(Pause for response.)* Yes, (Name) was chosen. But who's your real leader? *(Pause for response.)* Yes, God is! God already chose you to be his follower.

37

Our Changeless Christ

Scripture: Jesus Christ is the same yesterday and today and forever (Heb. 13:8).

Concept: Jesus never changes.

Object: A dead flower stalk, a few dead leaves or leaves that have changed color.

Look at what I picked up this week. *(Hold up the leaves and the flower stalk.)* They're a sure sign of autumn.

These leaves *(hold up the leaves)* were once green and lived on a tree. But now they've changed color, died, and fallen off.

This *(hold up the flower stalk)* was once a living flower. But it died. That happens this time of the year.

We see changes all around us during autumn, don't we? Trees lose their leaves, flowers die, birds fly farther south. The weather changes, we wear warmer clothes. Some people don't like these changes, but they can't be helped. Autumn is a time of change.

But then, there are always changes around us, aren't there? Grass becomes greener in the spring. The weather turns hotter in the summer. Flowers die in the fall. Cold rain or snow falls in the winter. The world keeps changing.

Everything changes, doesn't it? Things change. Your clothes wear out. Your TV doesn't work as well as it once did. Your bike becomes rusty.

People change. They grow up, they become old, they become ill, they become healthy again.

Families change. People get married. Old people die. Babies are born.

Our church changes, too. Some families move away. New families join the church. Old friends leave, new friends arrive.

Sometimes we like the changes, sometimes we don't. It's not nice to lose a friend, is it? *(Pause and shake your head.)* Of course not. Yet we can't help it. Everything changes.

Everything? *(Pause slightly.)* Everybody? *(Pause again.)* The Bible tells us that there is one person who never changes. Can you think of who that is? *(Pause for response.)* That's right, Jesus *(or* God)! The Bible says that Jesus Christ is the same yesterday, today, and forever. Jesus will never, ever change.

That's good, isn't it? *(Pause and nod your head.)* Of course it is! Jesus loves you and wants only the best for you. If he loves you today, he will love you tomorrow and forever. Jesus never changes, so he will always love you.

(Hold up the flower stalk and the leaves.) These are simply a signal of change in the weather. You can see all sorts of changes outside at this time of year. This week, look for all the changes you can find outside.

Every time you see a change outside you can remember the one thing that never changes. Jesus will always be the same. Jesus will love you forever.

38

Turn On Your Night-Light

ME VERSE: ...ame way, let your light shine ..., that they may see your good deeds and praise your Father in heaven (Matt. 5:16).

Concept: We let our lights shine by doing good deeds.

Object: A night-light. If you can, connect the light to a power source.

I wonder, how many of you have a night-light in your house? *(Hold up the night-light and pause for response.)* Sure, lots of people have night-lights at home.

When do you use a night-light? *(Pause for response.)* Of course, at night! Many people turn on a night-light when they turn off all the other lights. *(If you can, turn on the light.)*

A night-light helps us see in the dark. If we get up for some reason at night, we can see what we're doing and where we're going if a night-light is on. *(Turn off the light.)* We can't see that much in the dark; a night-light helps us see.

How many of you have your own night-light in your bedroom? *(Pause for response.)* Some do, some don't, but we all know what they are.

We don't all *have* night-lights, but we're all supposed to *be* night-lights. That's right! Jesus said that we are supposed to be lights; he didn't say night-lights *(hold up the night-light)*, but he did say lights. Jesus said that we should let our lights shine *(hold the light high and turn it on if you can)* to help people see God.

What can we do to help people see God? What can we do to help people think about God? *(Pause for response. Repeat responses.)* Tell people about God, yes. Invite people to church, yes.

Jesus told us one way everyone can let his or her light shine. He said that we should do good deeds *(hold up the light and turn it on)* so that people would see the good deeds and praise God.

That's a good way to let your light shine. Anyone can do good deeds if he or she tries. Even children like you can do good deeds. What kind of good deeds can you do? *(Pause for response and repeat responses.)* You can share toys, you can help with chores, you can be nice to someone who doesn't have friends, you can always have a cheerful word. You can do all sorts of good deeds.

When you do good deeds like those, people notice them. They know that you're a Christian, and God gets the praise for your good deeds. *(Hold up the night-light and turn it on.)* By your good deeds, you're letting your light shine so people can see God.

Jesus wants us all to let our lights shine by doing good deeds. We can all do good deeds, can't we? *(Nod your head and pause for response.)* Of course we can; but sometimes we need a reminder.

So, your night-light, or any light you turn on, can be your reminder. *(Hold up the night-light and turn it on.)* When you turn on the night-light to help you see, look at the way it shines in the dark. Its shining can remind you that Jesus wants us to let our lights shine by doing good deeds.

39

Dress for the Weather

Scripture: Put on the full armor of God so that you can take your stand against the devil's schemes (Eph. 6:11).

Concept: We should consciously equip ourselves to meet the challenges of the devil.

Objects: A pair of mittens, a jacket, a warm hat, or any three different pieces of clothing that people wear outside as the weather turns cooler.

How many of you wore a jacket or a coat to church this morning? *(Pause for response.)* So did I! The weather's cold outside, so we have to dress for it.

I've brought along some clothing we all probably wear during cold weather. *(Display the pieces of clothing as you speak.)* I need one person to put on some of these clothes. You'll all put on clothes like this many times this week, but now I need one person up here to do it. *(Pick a child and ask him or her to stand next to you.)*

First, we'll put on the jacket. *(Help the child put on the jacket as you speak.)* Why do we wear jackets in cold weather? *(Pause for response.)* Of course, to keep our bodies warm. Jackets cover the most important parts of our bodies; we have to keep our heart and lungs warm.

(Hold up the hat and help the child put it on as you speak.) Sometimes people don't like to wear a hat, but hats are very important. Can anyone tell me why? *(Pause for response.)* Doctors tell us that we lose a lot of our precious body heat through our heads. So we should wear hats to keep our heads warm.

(Hold up the mittens and help the child put them on as you speak.) Why do we wear mittens? *(Pause for response.)* Of course, we want to keep our hands and fingers warm. It's not fun to have cold, stiff fingers. And we certainly don't want them to freeze like icicles, do we? So we wear mittens.

There, (the child's name) is ready to go outside. It's cold out there, but he (*or* she) is protected now.

We all bundle up when we go outside in cold weather, don't we? Otherwise we might become ill. So we protect ourselves by putting on a jacket, a hat, and mittens.

(Keep the child standing by you as you speak.) Can we always see that it's cold out there? Can we always tell that we might become sick if we go out without bundling up? *(Shake your head and pause for response.)* Of course not! We can't see the cold. We just know that it's cold outside, so we should protect ourselves.

Did you know that God says we should protect ourselves when we go outside? *(Pause briefly for response.)* God doesn't say that we should wear a jacket, hat, and mittens when the weather is cold. He says something much more important.

God warns us that the world is not always good for Christians. Like cold weather for our bodies, the world can be bad for Christians. We can't always see what's bad for us, but God warns us that bad things are there.

God says that there is evil in the world; the devil wants to take us away from God. That would make us sick Christians.

So, God says, we should think about that danger and protect ourselves, just like (the child's name) is protected against the weather. Every time we go out into the world—among people who are not Christians—we should stop and think. We should say to ourselves, "It's not always good for me out there. How can I protect myself?" And then we should put on that protection just as we put on warm clothes.

What can we do to stay healthy as Christians? Maybe you can help me think of things. I'll give it a start.

(Take the hat off the child and show it to the children.) Just as we put on a hat, we can put on a prayer. Before we go into the world we can ask Jesus to keep us near him. That's putting on a prayer. Every time you see a hat, think of a prayer.

What else can we do? *(Pause for response. Repeat any responses and use them if possible. If not, use the following two.)* That's right, we can remind ourselves to act loving and good, as Jesus wants us to. *(Help the child remove the mittens.)* These mittens can remind us of good acts (*or* righteousness). When you put on mittens, think of putting on good acts.

Why don't we call the jacket *(help the child remove the jacket)* the jacket of God's love? We know that God loves us, but we should remind ourselves that he does every once in a while. So the jacket can remind you of God's love.

Now, let's dress as Christians for the outside world. *(Help the child put on the jacket once more.)* Every time you put on your jacket you can think of what? *(Pause for response.)* That's right, God's love! Remind yourself that God's love surrounds you.

(Help the child put on the mittens.) And what do the mittens stand for? *(Pause for response.)* That's right, righteousness or good acts. Every time you put on your mittens, remind yourself to do good acts or deeds for Jesus.

(Help the child put on the hat once more.) And never forget the important hat. What does it stand for? *(Pause for response.)* That's right, prayer! Always say a special prayer before you go out into the world. Always pray that God will keep you safe from evil.

Can you remember those things? This cold weather will help. Every time you protect yourself from the cold weather, remember to protect yourself from evil.

(Help the child take off the hat, mittens, and jacket quickly as you talk. Show them to the children once more as you refer to them.) Before you go out into the world, surround yourself with the jacket of *(pause slightly for response)* God's love. Put on the mittens of *(pause slightly)* good works. And above all, don't forget your hat of *(pause slightly)* prayer. And God, who watches over you in warm weather and cold, will keep you protected, safely close to him.

40

It's Not Fair!

(World Hunger)

Scripture: He has showed you, O man, what is good. And what does the LORD require of you? To act justly and to love mercy and to walk humbly with your God (Micah 6:8).

Concept: We should share.

Object: A box of raisins. You should have just enough raisins to give each child a handful.

I have some treats for you to take home today: raisins! *(Hold up the box, then pass out the raisins. Pass them out very haphazardly. Give large handfuls to some children, small amounts to others, only one raisin to others, and none to others. Continue to speak as you pass out the treats. Make sure you have none left in the box.)* Please don't eat them here. Just hold them in your hand and look at them. Try not to drop them when you go back to your seats. Just hold them while you're up here.

There, all the raisins are gone. Do you all have some treats? *(Pause for response.)* No? Didn't you get any raisins, (names of children)? That's not fair, is it?

What about you people who do have raisins? Do you all have about a handful? *(Pause for response.)*

143

No? You only have *one* raisin? *(Address previous question to a child with only one.)* Who else has only one raisin? *(Pause for response.)* That's not fair, is it?

Does anyone have a *whole lot* of raisins? Look around a little bit. Who thinks he or she has more raisins than anybody else? *(Pause for response.)* You *do* have a lot of raisins, don't you? That's not really fair, is it?

Well, it looks as if these raisins weren't passed out fairly. Some of you have lots of raisins, some have a few, and some have none. That's not fair, is it?

What shall we do about it? *(Pause for response. Repeat responses.)* You're right, we should share. Those of you who have lots of raisins should give some to the people who have none. Look at the people sitting near you. If they have fewer raisins than you, share with them. *(Give them time to share.)*

There, that's much better! Now everybody has about the same amount of raisins. Before you shared, it just wasn't fair, was it?

I passed out those raisins unfairly on purpose. I wanted you to think about being fair. I wanted you to think about sharing.

These are only small treats, raisins. Sometimes the treats you get are much bigger and much more important, like your meals, or your clothes, or your house. It's not always fair, the way those things are passed out.

Life isn't always fair. That's just the way it is. The world isn't perfect anymore. Some people have way too much, and some people don't have enough. It's not fair!

What do you think God wants us to do about it? *(Pause for response. Repeat responses.)*

The Bible says that we should act justly. That means that we should try to be fair. If something is not fair, we should try to make it fair.

If someone doesn't have enough food, what should we do? *(Pause for response.)* That's right, we should share with her. If someone doesn't have enough clothes, what should we do? *(Pause for response.)* That's right, we should share with him. If someone doesn't have a nice warm home, what should we do? *(Pause for response.)* That's right, we should share with her.

Sharing isn't easy, is it? It's hard for children to share. It's even hard for adults to share. Life will probably never be fair. It's hard to make everything completely fair.

In fact, I'm not sure that everyone has exactly the same amount of raisins. Look once more at your raisins, then see how many your neighbor has. Share if you have more. *(Pause briefly.)* There, that's probably about as fair as we're going to make it.

Just because it's hard to share, should we stop trying? *(Shake your head and pause for response.)* Of course not. God told us to act justly—to try to make things fair—so we'll keep trying.

At least now you all have some raisins, right? You may all take them back to your seats with you. In fact, you may want to share them with someone in your family. Life's not fair; we'll try to share.

41

Thank You

(Thanksgiving)

Scripture: Always giving thanks to God the
Father for everything, in the name of our
Lord Jesus Christ (Eph. 5:20).

Concept: Remember to say thank you to God
for our blessings.

Object: A little gift, e.g., penny, raisins, piece
of candy, for each child. A penny is used in
this lesson. (*Note:* This lesson can be used anytime as written. The option for use on Thanksgiving Day is included near the end of the
lesson.)

Look at what I brought for you! *(Show the
children the pennies.)* I have one penny for each of you.
I'll hand them out before you go back to your seats.

What should you always say when someone gives
you a gift? *(Pause for response.)* Of course, you should
say thank you. Even when someone gives you a very
small gift, it's only polite to say thank you.

Do we always say thank you for things that people
give us? *(Pause for response.)* Sometimes we forget,
don't we? Do we thank whomever cooks our meals
each time we eat? Do we always thank the person

who buys our clothes? *(Pause for response.)* No! It's natural to forget to say thank you for everything. Usually we say it only for special gifts. Although we're grateful for everything we have, we don't always say thank you to the people responsible.

How about God? Do we always remember to say thank you to God? *(Pause for response.)* No! God gives us everything we have, yet we don't always remember to say thank you to him.

Can you think of some things that God gives us? *(Pause for response. Prompt the children with questions.)* Food, yes! Do you say thank you to God for food? *(Pause for response.)* Yes, we often do. Does God give us our clothes? *(Pause for response.)* Yes, he does. Do you often say thank you to God for your clothes? *(Pause slightly.)* Most of us forget to, don't we? How about friends? Does God give us friends? *(Pause for response.)* Of course he does. Do you often thank God for your friends? *(Pause for response.)* We often forget to say thanks to God for friends, don't we?

(Continue in this manner as long as you feel you have time. Mention a gift from God, then ask if the children say thank you for that gift.)

Often we do say a little prayer of thanks. Before we eat we often thank God for our food. But sometimes we hardly think about what we say. Before we go to bed we pray and often thank God for being with us through the day. But sometimes we forget the thanks.

It's natural to forget. We're not perfect. We begin to expect God to give us things, and we sometimes forget to say thanks. God understands.

But still, it's good to remind ourselves to say thank you. It's good to take some time to make sure we thank God for his blessings.

Option

(Include the following paragraphs for use on Thanksgiving Day.)

Today is Thanksgiving, a special day to say thanks to God. And maybe this day can remind us to say thank you to him more often throughout the year.

I suppose most of you will have a big dinner today. And you may have company for dinner, or you may visit with friends or relatives today. There's going to be a lot of excitement and food. Don't forget to say thank you to God today. That's what the day is all about.

Continue Lesson

That's why I brought these pennies for you—to remind you to say thank you to God. Before you put this away (into a bank, eat it, *or whatever applies*), say a special thank you to God for all his blessings.

In fact, you can practice right now. When I give you the penny, say thank you aloud to me for practice. Then keep the penny with you for a while, and when you put it away, say thank you to God.

Try to remember always to say thank you, especially to God. *(Pass out the pennies after you are done speaking, so that everyone can hear the thank yous.)*

42

Almighty God

Memory Verse:

Scripture: I pray also that the eyes of your heart may be enlightened in order that you may know . . . his incomparably great power for us who believe (Eph. 1:18–19).

Concept: Only God is almighty.

Object: A doll or a picture of the most recent superhero, e.g., Power Rangers or Ninja Turtles.

Can anyone tell me what this is? *(Display the doll or picture and pause for response.)* That's right, it's a Mighty Morphin Power Ranger *(or whatever)*. It's one of the latest super-power characters. We see it advertised on TV, see the dolls in stores, (see the program on TV—*however they're advertised*).

I don't pay much attention to these toys; you can probably tell me about them. What do the Power Rangers do? *(Pause for response.)* Are they good? *(Pause for response.)* Are they smarter than people? *(Pause for response.)* Are they strong? How strong? *(Pause for response.)* Can they do lots of things that ordinary people can't do? *(Pause for response.)*

(Make sure the children can see the doll or the picture.) It sounds like we have a super powerful hero here.

The Power Ranger *(or whatever)* is stronger and faster and better than people. This is a real hero.

Tell me one more thing about this Mighty Morphin Power Ranger. Is it real? Is there really a Power Ranger? *(Pause for response.)* No! The Power Ranger is pretend, isn't it? It's imaginary. No person or thing is all-powerful and can do all things.

Now, wait a minute. I said that no person is all-powerful and can do all things. Is that true? *(Shake your head and pause for response.)* No!

There's one person who really is all-powerful and really can do all things. Who is that? *(Pause for response.)* That's right, God!

The Bible tells us that God has incomparably great power. We can't compare God's power to anything on earth. It is greater than anything we know.

(Hold up the doll or picture again.) The Power Ranger is make believe, but God is real. God's power is real. Our God can do anything. If this Power Ranger were real, would God's power be greater? *(Pause for response.)* Yes! God's power is greater than anything on earth, real or make believe.

So, when you see *(or* see ads for*)* or hear about Power Rangers, go ahead and have a little fun. Pretend that they're really powerful and good. But then remind yourself that this *(hold up the Power Ranger)* is only imaginary; it's pretend.

Your Power Ranger can remind you that we know there really is someone who is all-powerful. That's your God, who really lives and can do anything. Isn't it great to have an all-powerful God?

43

Earthly Treasures

Scripture: Do not store up for yourselves treasures on earth, where moth and rust destroy, and where thieves break in and steal. But store up for yourselves treasures in heaven, where moth and rust do not destroy, and where thieves do not break in and steal. For where your treasure is, there your heart will be also (Matt. 6:19–21).

Concept: Don't become too attached to earthly treasures.

Object: A package of tinsel, enough so that each child can have some.

Who can tell me what this is? *(Hold up some tinsel and pause for response.)* That's right, it's tinsel. We see quite a bit of it just before Christmas.

What do we usually do with tinsel? *(Pause for response.)* Yes, we put it on our Christmas trees. At least some people do. Not everyone uses tinsel on his or her trees; but I'm sure we've all seen it.

I think it looks pretty on a Christmas tree. It reflects the lights, and it seems to glitter all by itself. It makes a tree look rich and expensive. It looks like real silver falling off the Christmas tree.

Is it real silver? Is this tinsel really a precious, expensive metal? *(Shake your head and pause for response.)* No! Tinsel is really quite cheap. It's not heavy metal, it's just skinny strips of foil.

In fact, this tinsel doesn't last very long, does it? When we take our Christmas trees down, do we keep the tinsel or do we usually throw it away? *(Pause for response.)* We usually throw it away, don't we? It's such cheap, lightweight stuff—not at all like real silver—that we dump it when we take down our trees. This tinsel isn't going to last more than a month *(or however long until most Christmas trees come down).*

Tinsel looks nice, it grabs your attention, and it makes a tree look rich; but it's really not worth very much. Enjoy it while it's up, but remember that it won't last long.

This tinsel reminds me of a lot of things we see around Christmas. A lot of them look really great. Sometimes we almost can't wait until we get some of the games or toys or (name one of the hottest items of the year) we see. They look really good to us. But we've got to remember that they're not going to last. They're only toys; they're only earthly treasures.

Jesus talks about earthly treasures in the Bible. He says that we shouldn't become too attached to our earthly treasures, we shouldn't love our toys and games and clothes too much. They don't last forever; they fall apart, they wear out, and soon they are dumped. Jesus says not to set our hearts on these things, not to treasure them too much.

152

Instead, Jesus says we should set our hearts on things that last forever. We should think about Jesus, and God, and heaven. We should thank God for his love and try to show love. We should store up the treasure of God's love for us.

Storing up treasures in heaven doesn't mean that we can't enjoy our Christmas presents, does it? *(Shake your head and pause for response.)* Of course not. You probably will get some nice things for Christmas; enjoy them.

But remember that they don't last. What does last is Jesus, whose birthday we celebrate at Christmas. Jesus' love is the most important part of Christmas; it's a true heavenly treasure.

Remember that I said this tinsel reminds me of a lot of earthly treasures we see around Christmas? *(Hold up the tinsel again.)* We can enjoy them, but they don't last.

I'd like to give each one of you some tinsel. *(Pass out the tinsel as you speak.)* Don't drop it. Carry it carefully. Try to take it all the way home with you. Then, you can put it on your Christmas tree at home. Every time you look at your tinsel, you can enjoy it, but remember that it's just an earthly treasure; it won't last.

When your family takes down your Christmas tree after Christmas, I'd like you to take that tinsel off and throw it away. Throwing it away will remind you of all earthly treasures; they all disappear sometime. And then you can think of the heavenly treasure that you have, and you can thank God for Jesus and his love.

44

Lost in a Crowd

Scripture: For I am convinced that neither death nor life, neither angels nor demons, neither the present nor the future, nor any powers, neither height nor depth, nor anything else in all creation, will be able to separate us from the love of God that is in Christ Jesus our Lord (Rom. 8:38–39)

Concept: Nothing can separate us from God.

Object: A picture of a crowd of people.

How many of you have gone to the mall (*or* a store) with your mom or dad lately? *(Pause for response.)* We all have to go shopping sometime. Lots of people go the mall (*or* a store).

I saw a picture this week that reminds me of the mall. *(Hold up the picture.)* You can't see the stores or the mall, can you? But you surely can see a crowd of people! That's why this picture reminds me of the mall. There are crowds of people at the mall.

When you're in a crowd like this, what do your mom or dad say to you? Do they say, "Hold my hand," or "Stay close to me"? *(Pause for response.)* Of course, your parents want to keep you close to their sides.

(Hold up the picture.) If you're in a crowd like this and you wander away from Mom or Dad, what can happen? Can you become lost? *(Pause for response.)* Yes, it's really easy to get lost in a crowd like this.

Just imagine yourself in the middle of this crowd trying to find Mom or Dad. That's a scary thought, isn't it? You never want to get lost in a crowd like this. That's why Mom and Dad want you to stay close or hold their hands. They don't want you to become separated from them. Hang on tightly; don't get separated; then you won't get lost in the crowd.

I don't want to scare you. But lots of people crowd stores and malls. *(Hold up the picture.)* When you're in a crowd, stick close to Mom and Dad so that you won't become separated from them.

There's someone else that you don't ever want to become separated from, someone who made you and loves you and wants you with him forever. Who is that? *(Pause for response.)* God! That's right, God loves you and wants you as his child forever.

We don't ever want to be separated from God, do we? *(Shake your head and pause for response.)* No! We know that he loves us and cares for us. We don't ever want to be separated from his love and care. It's scary to think about being separated from God.

I don't want to scare you, so we won't think about it anymore. We don't have to worry about being separated from God or from his love. God has told us that *nothing* can separate us from him. He tells us in the Bible that angels or demons, death or life, present or future, nothing in all of creation can separate us from his love *(hold up the picture and keep it up)*—not even a crowd of people like this. Absolutely nothing can separate us from God. He's promised us that.

But a crowd of people like you see in this picture, like you see at the mall, can separate us from Mom or Dad. So, the next time you go out into a crowd with them, hold their hands and stick close to them. You don't want to become separated from them.

And when you take their hands, imagine that you are also holding God's hand. That can remind you of what God has promised you: Nothing will ever separate you from his love.

45

The Message of Christmas

(Christmas)

Scripture: Here is a trustworthy saying that deserves full acceptance: Christ Jesus came into the world to save sinners (1 Tim. 1:15).

Concept: Jesus was born to save us.

Objects: A few Christmas cards, one Christmas card with the words of 1 Timothy 1:15 written inside. (*Note:* This lesson can be used on Christmas or anytime during the Christmas season.)

Is your family receiving lots of Christmas cards? *(Pause slightly.)* Look at all the cards I've gotten. *(Display a handful of cards.)* Most of these come from friends and relatives who just want to say hello at Christmas.

Most friends want to say more than just hello. I haven't heard from some of them for almost a year. Sometimes they add a letter to the card. Sometimes they pick a card with a really nice printed message. There's always some sort of message in these cards. I read them because they're messages from people I love.

Let's read some of them now. *(Open a few cards, read the printed messages, and name the person who sent the card.)*

How many of you have received Christmas cards with messages? *(Pause for response. If a child responds positively, ask who sent the card and if he or she remembers the message.)* I'm sure that your family has received some Christmas cards.

Pretend for a minute that you received a Christmas card from God. *(Hold up the card with the verse written inside.)* You open the card to see the message *(open the card)* . . . and what do you think the message would say? Would it say "Merry Christmas and Happy New Year"? Would it be "Santa Claus is coming"? I don't think so.

I think God would send a better Christmas message than that. If you got a Christmas card from God, what would God say to you? *(Pause for response. Repeat the children's responses. You may have to prompt them with questions.)* Would it be "I love you"? Would it be "Jesus was born"? Would it be "Here's my Son, the baby Jesus"? Maybe. A Christmas message from God could be any of those messages, couldn't it?

Here's what my pretend Christmas card from God says. Listen closely to the message. *(Read the verse.)* Is that a good Christmas message? *(Nod and pause for response.)* Of course! That message came from the Bible; that message came from God.

On Christmas we celebrate Jesus' birth. God sent the baby Jesus into the world to save sinners. Jesus was born to save us. That's the real message of Christmas. That's God's message to us. *(Hold up the "Christmas card from God.")*

These other Christmas cards are fine. *(Hold up the other Christmas cards.)* It's nice to stay in touch with loved ones and hear from them. They don't always give us the real message of Christmas: Jesus was born to save us. But it's still nice to get cards from friends and relatives.

And now, those Christmas cards can mean even more to you. When you see Christmas cards at your house this week, ask an adult to read them to you. Listen to the message on each card and think for a minute about the person who sent it. Then think about getting a Christmas card from God *(hold up the card)* and remember the message that God sends you on Christmas: Jesus was born to save us.